G.O.1

MW01172737

For

Arresting Allergies

First Edition

A Publication of:

M.E.E.T. Ministry

Missionary Education and Evangelistic Training
480 Neely Lane
Huntingdon, TN 38344
Phone (731) 986-3518
Fax (731) 986-0582
E-mail: godsplan@meetministry.org
Web Site: www.meetministry.org

About the Cover

CONTRIBUTIONS

GOD'S PLAN

God

Manuscript
Lynn Neeley
Thomas Jackson

Research Contributions
Thomas Jackson
Lynn Neeley

Art and Layout
Joan Frank
Joya Jones
Layout and design

Dea Davis
Cover Design

Review and Editing
Janice Maywether

Health and Happiness
Library Series

"Sickness abounds for want of sound, practical life-style education. I have grown to appreciate your emphasis on the simple life-style principles given in the Bible which contain the therapeutic properties handcrafted by the Creator. GOD'S PLAN is indeed the best plan. Keep up the good work." R. Blackburn, M.D., Texas

"The health and happiness library series has really helped me understand more about GOD'S PLAN for health. I have been able to help many people in my country using the simple remedies found in nature. I look forward to the other books in this series." F. Sue, Registered Nurse, Taiwan

"I have appreciated the simple biblical approach to health that M.E.E.T. ministry promotes through its publications. The eight laws of health have been a spiritual, mental and physical blessing to my congregation." R. Gale, Pastor, Tennessee

Important!

The information presented in this book is based on God's original life-style plan as it is presented in the Holy Bible. This information is provided for educational purposes only and is not intended as treatment for an individual's health concerns or ailments.

Furthermore, the information in this book is not intended as either medical advice, diagnosis, or prescription. The publisher assumes no responsibility for any adverse conditions or consequences that may result from the use or misuse of the information presented in this book.

Table of Contents

Dear Reader,

This booklet was written with you in mind because we care about you, and we want you to experience the health and happiness that our Creator designed for you to have, and also, about the remedies which God gave you free of charge to keep you in good health. Enjoy your reading, and if you have any comments or questions, feel free to contact us. Our address and phone number are listed on page one. Let us know how we can serve you. We are praying that everyone who reads this booklet, as well as any other booklets in our **HEALTH AND HAPPINESS LIBRARY SERIES,** will find in the eight simple remedies **GOD'S PLAN FOR THE PRESERVATION AND RESTORATION OF HEALTH.**

Yours in Christ,

M.E.E.T. Ministry Publishing

Introduction

One promise which is not understood or claimed is found in the Bible in *Exodus 15:26. If thou wilt diligently hearken to the voice of the Lord thy God, and wilt do that which is right in His sight, and wilt give ear to His commandments, and keep all His statutes, I will put none of these diseases upon thee, which I have brought upon the Egyptians, for I am the Lord that healeth thee."*

This promise is so significant, particularly when one realizes what types of diseases the Egyptians suffered from. Incredibly, they are the same diseases that many Americans are experiencing now. Paleopathologists (those who study ancient diseases), have uncovered numerous mummies which were contemporaries of the Biblical era. The mummies revealed that the Egyptians suffered from many of the same diseases, which plague Americans now. Cancer, heart disease, diabetes, arthritis, allergies, obesity and numerous other illnesses were found. Does this amazing promise from Exodus still hold true? Unequivocally, YES! God tells us in *Malachi 3:6* that, *"I am the Lord, I change not...."* Do we believe this?

Here in Exodus, God has provided a conditional promise, conditional in that we are told that we have a part to play. Our part is to *"hearken to the voice of the Lord...and do that which is right in His sight."* God's part is to *"put none of these diseases upon thee which I have brought upon the Egyptians."* Why will we be free from these diseases? *"I am the Lord that healeth thee."* There are very simple laws of health that God has instructed us to follow. If these laws were followed, the suffering and disease which plague so many today would be markedly diminished.

Approximately 50 million Americans suffer with what is commonly called hay fever or allergies.[1] Also known as seasonal allergic rhinitis, this ailment results in an annual loss of 3.5 million workdays and 2 million schooldays.[2], 16.7 million office visits to medical providers are attributed to allergies.[3] It is the most common chronic condition in childhood[4] and the sixth leading chronic disease in adults according to the American Academy of Allergy, Asthma, and Immunology.[5]

It is felt that over 40% of all cases of sinusitis is due to allergies;[6] and in 1996, chronic sinusitis was the most commonly reported chronic disease, affecting approximately 38 million people in the United States and costing more than $5.8 billion.[7] What is even more interesting is a study revealing that while 50% of adults recognize the source of their allergies within five years, more than 22% endure this illness for more than fifteen years before they find the cause.[8]

One third of the population, it is estimated, will develop allergies at some point in their life. Forty percent of school children have at least one allergy, and twenty percent of children have asthma, a "cousin" of allergies. The proportion of the population with allergies increased throughout the 20th century from 1% to nearly 50% from 1920 to 2000. The odds are high that you or someone in your family is affected by allergic symptoms.[9]

Food allergies are also definitely on the rise. This rapid increase began in 1970. Some physicians estimate that at least 60% of the US population suffers from symptoms associated with food intolerance.[10] *Time* magazine conservatively estimates that approximately seven million Americans suffer from food allergies and that this year, "some three hundred thousand will develop reactions severe enough to send them to the emergency ward, and about two hundred will die." Unfortunately, some reactions can even be triggered by not actually ingesting a substance, but merely kissing someone who has eaten the food to which you are allergic.[11]

Why this increase in the last portion of the 20th century? What can be done to prevent the chance of developing an allergy? What can one do if an allergy already exists? The Bible, the instruction manual for life, states in *Proverbs 26:2*, **"the curse causeless shall not come."**

There are numerous products that promise to relieve, alleviate or control an allergy. They all promise a quick fix. But is it really a fix, or rather, an illusion? Is this truly the only option? Must life be filled with a constant dread of the offending substance? Francis Bacon once said, "A healthy body is a guest-chamber for the soul; a sick body is a prison."[12] There is such a difference between controlling a substance and actually experiencing wellness! The fact is that one CAN get well from allergies without using drugs! GOD'S PLAN is for fullness of joy, with life and health abundant.

The Fence or the Ambulance

Twas a dangerous cliff as they freely confessed,
Though to walk near its crest was so pleasant;
But over its terrible edge there had slipped
A duke and many a peasant;
So the people said something would have to be done,
But their projects did not at all tally:
Some said, "Put a fence round the edge of the cliff";
Some, "An ambulance down in the valley."

But the cry for the ambulance carried the day,
For it spread to the neighboring city;
A fence may be useful or not, it is true,
But each heart became brimful of pity
For those who had slipped o'er that dangerous cliff,
And the dwellers in highway and alley
Gave pounds or gave pence, not to put up a fence,
But an ambulance down in the valley.

"For the cliff is all right if you're careful," they said;
"And if folks even slip or are dropping,
It isn't the slipping that hurts them so much
As the shock down below - when they're stopping."
So day after day when these mishaps occurred,
Quick forth would the rescuers sally
To pick up the victims who fell off the cliff
With their ambulance down in the valley.

Then an old man remarked: "It's a marvel to me
That people give far more attention
To repairing results than to stopping the cause,
When they'd much better aim at prevention.

Let us stop at its source all this mischief," cried he,
"Come neighbors and friends, let us rally;
If the cliff we will fence, we might almost dispense
With the ambulance down in the valley."

"Oh, he's a fanatic," the others rejoined;
"Dispense with the ambulance? Never!
He'd dispense with all charities, too, if he could;
No, no! We'll support them forever.
Aren't we picking up folks just as fast as they fall?
And shall this man dictate to us? Shall he?
Why should people of sense stop to put up a fence,
While their ambulance works in the valley?"

Thus this story so old has beautifully told
How our people with best of intentions,
Have wasted their years and lavished their tears
On treatment, with naught for prevention.

But a sensible few, who are practical too,
Will not bear with such nonsense much longer;
They believe that prevention is better than cure
And their party will soon be the stronger.
Encourage them, then, with your purse, voice, and pen,
And (while other philanthropists dally)
They will scorn all pretense, and put up a stout fence
On the cliff that hangs over the valley.
                                    -Joseph Malines

THE NATURE OF ALLERGIES

"Give me understanding, and I shall keep thy law, yea , I shall observe it with my whole heart."   *Psalm 119:34.*

What is an allergy? An allergy is "A collection of symptoms caused by an immune response to substances that do not trigger an immune response in most people."[13] According to Taber's Medical Dictionary, an allergy is "an acquired hypersensitivity to a substance (allergen) that does

not normally cause a reaction." In other words, allergies consist of symptoms that occur as a response to some substance referred to as an allergen. The offending substance does not cause a reaction in most people and only occurs after at least one prior exposure.

The immune system, which was created by God to fight infection or foreign material, is responsible for this reaction. It destroys all foreign invaders, as well as abnormal cells that the body may produce in growth or repair, known as cancer cells. It protects our bodies throughout the day from a constant assault, of which we are usually unaware. Those with allergies, have an immune system that is responding to things "that are generally harmless and in most people do not cause an immune response."[14] What an allergy is really saying, is that the person, for a variety of possible reasons, has a compromised immune system as well as a toxic system, and no longer has the normal ability to cope appropriately with the allergen.

The word allergy was coined in 1906 from two Greek words meaning a reaction of the immune system to foreign matter, which results in detrimental, rather than beneficial, effects on the host. The term also implies exposure to the substance prior to the negative affect. It has been extremely difficult to perform research in this area. How does one study something that seems to cause a headache in one person, rashes in another, depression in still another and nothing in the remainder?

In 1926, European and American physicians agreed to limit the term allergy to reactions that had a measurable immune response; reactions only that caused an antibody reaction that could be measured in a laboratory. In 1967, a specific antibody called IgE was discovered which further reinforced the idea of having a concrete measurable result. From 1926 on, there have been two schools of thought on the diagnosis and treatment of allergies. Allergists themselves though, do not all agree on the necessity of a measurable immune response to be present, as stated by Drs. Fireman and Slavin in the *Atlas of Allergies*.[15] There is a growing realization that the immune system is often influenced indirectly, as we will discuss further.

Normal body cells have a special coating that signals to the white blood cells (the fighter cells for the immune system) in the body that they are supposed to be there. Foreign substances and dead tissue do not have this special coating and are engulfed and removed (eaten) by white blood cells. Antibodies may be produced when a foreign substance enters into the body. These antibodies attach to mast cells, which are large cells that are located near blood vessels. The next time the allergen is in contact with the body, the immune system immediately recognizes it and attacks. The mast cell is altered and releases histamine, which may cause blood vessels to dilate (the skin appears red and warm), smooth muscles to contract (difficulty breathing), and/or tissues to become edematous (swell). These symptoms may occur in a matter of minutes or hours; sometimes, it may even be days depending on the type of cell that responds. The reaction occurs from the release of histamine or histamine-like substances from injured cells.[16, 17]

What many people would readily recognize as an allergic reaction, may also be occurring in the body in a place where there are no nerve endings, thus the person is oblivious that there is an inflammatory reaction occurring. The same inflammatory reaction of redness and swelling with warmth may still be occurring, only the person is unaware.

This is just one of many ways that the immune system may react with allergies. An allergy may react with the immune system directly, as outlined above with the allergen/antibody complex, or it may react indirectly with the immune system. An example of an indirect reaction, one that occurs outside of the immune system, is food intolerance. When one eats food that does not digest completely, the undigested and thus rather large protein may be absorbed into the blood stream. There may not be a direct increase in antibodies. One may exhibit gastrointestinal distress and be labeled as having food intolerance. Fortunately, the body continues to attempt to maintain normal function or homeostasis. The blood may carry these absorbed, undigested proteins to any part of the body. While this intolerance may not fit the allergist's narrow definition requiring antibodies to be present, the immune system is still involved in an attempt to remove the foreign protein. This indirectly drains the immune system. **ALL** allergies stress the immune system; it is just a matter of when and how.

Many advise avoiding trigger foods, but that is only a partial solution, as many foods have cross-reactions with other foods from the same food group. For example, many that are allergic to peanuts are also allergic to pinto beans. Enhancement of the immune system is the key.

Attempting to treat an airborne allergy by moving to a new location is not the answer. Eventually you will simply develop a new set of allergies to the new environment. The answer to either reaction is strengthening the immune system, as we will discuss later. *"No man can enter into a strong man's house, and spoil his goods, except he will first bind the strong man; and then he will spoil his house." Mark 3:27.* It is essential that the "strong man"(in this case the immune system), be free to ward off any potential uninvited and unwelcomed invaders.

The possibilities of symptoms, which may occur as a result of an allergy, are multiple, and may vary according to the allergen (that which provokes the allergic response). What one must realize is that these symptoms are the cumulative result of overwhelming the immune system, and if allowed to continue over a period of months and years, can be responsible for opening the door to other life-threatening diseases by the constant drain on the immune system. One interesting concept is that allergies do not cause every disease, but they may be an influence resulting in more serious forms of diseases. Allergies are not just a nuisance![18]

Symptoms of an allergy include, but are not limited to, a runny nose, increased tearing, and itching of the nose, mouth, eyes, throat, skin, or any other area. Wheezing, coughing, shortness of breath, redness of the skin, hives, skin rashes, stomach cramps, vomiting, diarrhea, feeling bloated, hearing loss, ear discharges/bleeding and/or headaches are other symptoms. Also included are sneezing, sore throat, bronchial and sinus infections, asthma, insomnia, menstrual disorders, hypoglycemia, bedwetting, tinnitus (ringing in the ears), failure to thrive (or grow), joint pain, canker sores, and learning disorders.[19] Studies have even shown a relationship with glaucoma and allergies.[20] Menopausal symptoms, due to the respiratory center in the brain being suppressed, may result in an increased heat production and the infamous "night sweats" from allergies.[21] As a result of an allergy, one may become a mouth breather due to the constant stuffy nose. After many years, one may develop "allergic shiners," (dark areas around the eye), or a crease on the bridge of the nose from the "allergic salute" - pushing the nose upward with the palm of the hand

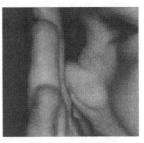

to rub the nose.[22] Any chronic cold, cough or nosebleed may be a result of an allergen. A child will often pick their nose in an effort to clear the nose, or twitch it like a rabbit to clear obstruction.

Allergic reactions can resemble the symptoms of almost any disease. They can affect how people feel, act and even think. They are not just limited to physical ills, but they can also affect the mind. *Annals of Allergies* report remarkable improvement in attitude after removal of milk and chocolate from a teenager's diet in just forty-eight hours. Physical appearance improved, as well as alertness, cheerfulness and interest in the surroundings.[23] Depression, hyperactivity, irritability, nervousness, paranoia, apathy and stammering are a few neurological symptoms that have resolved after successfully eliminating allergies. Although some symptoms resolve immediately after the removal of the offending substance, some require up to three weeks for a change in behavior.[24]

Dr. James Braly, the director of Immuno Laboratories in Florida, is one of several physicians who have noted the relationship between many diseases and allergies. He estimates that eighty medical conditions either have their basis or are contributed to by allergies or food sensitivities.[25]

CAUSES OF ALLERGIES
"The cause which I knew not, I searched out." Job 29:19.

Causes of allergies are as multiple, as are the symptoms. What affects one may not affect another. Why? **Heredity** is an important factor as is a person's metabolic state or vital force. Some people innately are able to cope with stressors with a much lower nutrient demand than others are. All **stress** requires extra nutrients, but for some, the required nutrients for just maintenance of optimal health are higher.

It is believed that a person does not inherit an actual allergy, but rather, a tendency to allergies or a predisposition to an allergy. The chances of a child becoming allergic increase 50-60% if a parent has an allergy. If both parents have allergies, the child's chances of developing an allergy increase to 67-100%. Fetal blood has been found to have an increased level of IgE, an immunoglobulin, which increases when allergies are present. Increased levels of IgE are present as early as eleven weeks of gestation in the liver and lungs of fetal tissue, if allergies are present. This IgE is not found in the arterial blood of the umbilical cord. It is therefore believed that it must have a fetal, not maternal source. Allergies to penicillin, wheat, milk and eggs have been documented as being transferred, by the allergen, to the fetus, resulting in hypersensitivity from birth.[26] Allergies therefore may be present from birth.

Children born in September, October or November have a higher risk of allergies than those born in June, July, and August. It is thought that this could be related to the amount of **time the infant spends indoors** during the colder months, resulting in greater exposure to house dust. Dr. A. Thrash also notes "high humidity, fatigue, cold weather, and chilling may lower tolerance to allergens."[27]

East German children were followed after the fall of communism, and were noted to have a dramatic increase in allergies in general and hay fever in particular, as they were exposed to western living. This supports the theory of some allergists that **affluence** also has played a role in the increase of allergies. Feeding a **baby formula instead of breast milk** has been associated with increased incidence of allergies, as well as rapid weaning of infants to solid foods. Unfortunately, there is a direct relationship with affluence and decreased breast-feeding.

With **aging**, the immune system is weakened. This can result from poor dietary habits, physical, environmental or emotional stress, or the cumulative affect of all of the above. This increased demand of nutrients, in addition to the decreased enzymes available on a typical Standard American Diet (S.A.D.) and decreased nutrient absorption that often occurs with aging, is one reason that allergies may increase with age.

So what else can actually cause the allergy? There are four major disease-causing organisms: **bacteria, viruses, parasites and mold/fungi.** One is exposed to these organisms on a daily basis and is usually assaulted by an attack from the immune system. The body may be overly sensitive to airborne allergens like pollen, spores, and molds. These organisms

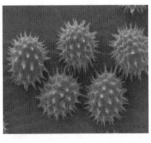

react with excess mucous and waste, that rather than being eliminated, have accumulated in the body. They also may result in increased mucus production. Lifestyle is usually responsible for this toxic accumulation.

Many people are allergic to mold. Molds are microscopic living organisms that are beneficial. They assist in the decomposition of compost and leaves, and fertilize gardens. Molds, however, are harmful to humans; unfortunately flourishing in air, soil or organic matter. Thriving in dark moist places and flourishing in summer and fall, mold is often windborne. Bottled water may also contain mold. Molds produce and release into the air antibiotics, which can damage tissue cells, in particular nerve cells. Molds also can increase the number of allergic reactions one has, as well as influence their severity. Molds have been found to be responsible for more respiratory infections than bacteria and this in persons with apparently "normal" immunity.[28]

Bacteria, viruses, and all chronic parasitic infections not only release toxins into the body that must be eliminated, but compete with nutrients and overwork the immune system. Parasite cleansing is important! Many of these toxins are similar to substances produced in the body after ingesting alcohol.

As energy efficient homes have increased, as well as the number of urban dwellers, we have seen an increase in **indoor air pollutants**. House dust, tobacco smoke, nitrogen dioxide, and ozone are just a few. Urban dwellers are breathing an inordinate amount of ozone. The American Lung Association's State of the Air Report states that there are "more than 142 million Americans residing in counties in which the air contains unhealthy levels of ozone air pollution...This is the third consecutive year during which at least half of the country's population breathed unhealthy air." [29]

Formaldehyde, which is used in plywood, fiberboard, dry-cleaned clothing, and carpet backing, is a major culprit. Studies have linked formaldehyde to vitamin B6 deficiency. Plastics, insulation materials, glues, paints, synthetic fibers and fabrics, deodorizers, aerosols, faulty air conditioners and humidifiers, gas stoves, heaters, fireplaces that use energy saving inserts, wood burning stoves, kerosene-burning heaters and radon are additional pollutants.

Recently, the CDC released a report that focused on 116 chemicals polluting the environment. These range from dioxins and PCB to lead and second-hand tobacco smoke that was measured in urine and/or blood. Their focus now, is finding the safe upper limit of these chemicals, which, in the opinion of many, should rather be labeled poisons. Again, the emphasis needs to be total avoidance when possible, and strengthening the body, in particular, the immune system.[30]

Insecticide spraying is another factor. This may affect children

exposed during school hours, and while playing in public sandboxes. Fortunately, some states are beginning to require schools to notify parents when spraying is to occur.

If your child complains of headaches or unusual smells at school, the school may be a "sick building" and may need to be investigated. Look for dampness, paint smells or water stains. If your children must ride the bus to school, instruct them to sit at the front of the bus, and to ask the driver to keep the windows open.

There are web sites with helpful information if you feel that your child's school is a factor.

Some **pets**, their skin, scales or danders, as well as their wastes, are other factors. Pets should remain outside if possible and if indoors should have specific boundaries and definitely not be allowed in sleeping quarters. Surprisingly, allergens have even been found in large numbers on driver's seats of vehicles, even in automobiles of non-pet owners. These  allergens are from your neighbor's pets and attach themselves to your clothes. They are then transferred to your vehicle or furniture. One particular study found that although vehicle levels were not high enough to cause symptoms, clothing levels were.[31]

Other possible causes of allergies include specific organ damage or stress. **Adrenal exhaustion** from multiple stressors, **essential fatty acids deficiency** (fats that are necessary for proper cell functions), and destructive molecular fragments that damage the cells, called **free radicals**, which lowers antihistamine levels and liver function, are just a few other contributing factors.[32] There are several research studies of leukotrienes, (biochemicals that maintain inflammatory conditions after they are triggered), prostaglandins and antioxidants. They trigger undesired vasoactive and inflammatory responses that are one of the main causes of the allergy and asthma symptoms.

It is currently felt that adrenal exhaustion may be inherited to some degree. Dr. James Wilson states that if "one or both parents suffer from adrenal fatigue, either chronically or during the time of conception, and if the mother has adrenal fatigue during gestation, there is a greater than 50% chance that their children will also suffer from adrenal fatigue. This may be seen as a child with a weak constitution, early allergies, a propensity toward lung infections, and a decreased ability to handle stress..."[33]

In one study, all of the cases of a group of children suffering from symptoms of food allergies showed evidence of an **imbalance of bowel bacteria**. Specifically, deficiencies of Lactobacillus and Bifidobacteria combined with Enterobacteriaceae overgrowth were found.[34] Lactobacillus and Bifidobacteria are two of the many normal bacteria that are found in a healthy digestive tract. A variety of lifestyle practices, as basic as improper chewing, can alter the digestive tract and result in the Enterobacteriaceae overgrowth.

Candida albicans overgrowth, caused by an imbalance of the normal, healthy bacteria that is found in the digestive tract, results in a condition that is commonly referred to as candidiasis. Overuse of antibiotics and/or steroids as well as the use of birth control pills, are some of many factors that may lead to candida. Many feel that the amount of antibiotics that they have taken is not excessive. The amount of antibiotics that are routinely used in dairy and meat production is not common knowledge. Seventy percent of cattle, in the United States, receive antibiotics, which, if ingested, affect the human body. The normal bacteria in the intestine are killed and an environment is produced in which the candida yeast can grow out of control.

This fungal form can eventually penetrate into the walls of the intestines as well as other tissue. This may increase the permeability (leakage) of the intestines to incompletely digested proteins and may eventually result in what is termed "leaky gut syndrome," a term used to describe contents of the bowel leaking into the blood stream, thereby harming the system. When this bacterial imbalance is present, nutrients are utilized by the fungi, which should be feeding the cells of the body. Diets that are high in carbohydrates and low in certain nutrients only aid in the growth, as the immune system does not have the arsenal to adequately fight and to maintain the proper balance. The resulting toxins (more than one hundred identified so far[35]) released, inhibit the immune system (particularly the T cells) and may interfere with healthy metabolism. These toxins include acetaldehyde, a relative of formaldehyde and a byproduct from alcohol ingestion. They interfere with red blood cell flexibility and acetlycholine, a neurotransmitter, and may result in a chronic "hung-over" feeling."[36]

Unfortunately the lining of the intestine becomes weakened by the yeast and allows allergenic foods and incompletely digested proteins to enter the bloodstream. By changing the diet and lifestyle, temporary supplementation of healthy bacteria commonly referred to as probiotics, eliminating steroids, antibiotics, and other medicines which may increase its growth, as well as temporarily avoiding foods which will feed the candida, healthy intestinal flora may be restored.

The importance of temporary supplementation with beneficial bacteria aids digestion, as well as elimination. This supplementation may be in the form of live juices or herbs, which facilitate a proper bacteria balance, as well as oral or rectal bacteria supplementation. Severity of allergies is diminished and the intestinal walls are strengthened. There is a stronger resistance to toxins and microbes.[37] Toxins are one of the by-products that are released by the yeast, which also can be overwhelming to the immune system.

If one has intolerance to cheese, wine, beer, or highly concentrated sweets, one probably has candida. A diagnosis of candida is difficult to ascertain, but there are many questionnaires available which should raise the level of suspicion of whether this is a potential contributor to allergy episodes, as there is such a high cross-correlation between allergies and candida.

Food is another major source of allergies. As previously mentioned, researchers and physicians continue to debate whether food sensitivities without immune system involvement truly exists. The Academy of Allergy and Immunology divides food allergies into many subtypes, including food hypersensitivity, food anaphylaxis, food intolerance, food poisoning, and adverse reaction to a food. The majority of food allergies are cyclic, meaning that after avoiding the food for approximately four months, building the immune system and cleansing the body of toxins, they may be resumed with moderate intake.

When offending foods are temporarily removed and then reintroduced into the diet without rebuilding the system, symptoms often will escalate. *Annals of Allergy,* reports a study in their January 1980 issue, that 87% of patients who had rheumatoid arthritis or osteoarthritis found that allergies caused their joint pain and swelling. It was stated that joint pain seemed to be a late manifestation of food  allergies. The problem is that there is often a delay of up to five days between the trigger food and symptoms.[38]

Many food allergies result from the overuse of specific foods, which deplete the body of specific digestive enzymes. This results in **incompletely digested proteins**. There are other causes of food-based foreign proteins, which the body does not recognize as food. The body has been designed by God to attack any unidentifiable protein particles. This useful plan allows the body to remove bacteria or viruses. Most food allergens are portions of poorly digested proteins. These undigested proteins are absorbed into the intestine, impeding the immune system. This results in a low-tolerance state and therefore long-term allergies, as well as other degenerative illnesses. Rotating foods and avoiding potential trigger foods to every four to fourteen days may adequately remove potential overload. This should only need to be done temporarily while allowing the body to heal, particularly if digestive enzymes are utilized. A properly functioning liver will aid in removing foreign proteins.

Interestingly, by simply chewing food adequately, protein digestion is increased. With adequate chewing, ninety-eight percent of proteins are absorbed as amino acids. The digestive tract is therefore not bombarded with large amounts of undigested proteins. The liquid food or chyme, instead of the large undigested proteins, is therefore able to pass rapidly, and without as much difficulty through the digestive tract with minimum symptoms from potential allergens.[39]

Intestinal absorption of large proteins can be a result of an immature gastrointestinal tract, decreased stomach acid, vitamin A deficiency, inadequate chewing, insufficient digestive enzymes or an inflammation of the intestinal tract. A bacterial, viral or yeast infection in the intestine, parasites, toxins, and radiation, such as may be used in cancer treatment, can damage the intestinal wall and cause increased absorption of partially digested particles. Overeating and eating a predominance of over-processed, refined foods, will facilitate enzyme deficiency.[40]

Insufficient enzymes are another major cause of allergies. There are more than 5,000 enzymes, which are proteins in the body that are essential for every process in the body. Some have estimated that it takes more than 100,000 enzymes for the body to function.[41] Some have estimated that 90% of all allergies could be eliminated if enzymes were properly used.

There are many types of enzymes that serve in different functions, but we will focus on digestive enzymes, which further break food down into small particles allowing nutrients to become available from our food.

Digestion begins in the mouth, which is why proper chewing is essential. The more the food is chewed the more surface area available for enzymes to begin the digestive process. As the food is moved into the stomach, digestion is continued, although at a different ph and for different portions of the food (carbohydrate versus fat versus protein). While the proper ph is being attained in the stomach, digestive enzymes from the mouth, now in the stomach, as well as the digestive enzymes naturally occurring in raw food, can digest 60% of the starch, 30% of the protein, and 10% of the fat in food. The University of Illinois conducted a study revealing that 80% of carbohydrates can be digested during this period, all before the stomach even begins the digestive process.[42] Hydrochloric acid is increasing in the stomach, changing the ph of the stomach, at which point the salivary enzymes are inactivated. This is all before the stomach digestive juices have been activated. After the stomach completes its portion of digestion, the process is then continued in the small intestine where salivary enzymes are reactivated. The bottom line is that the better the food is chewed and the higher the percentage of raw food eaten, the more enzymes there will be available. This benefits more than digestion.

For one who eats predominately cooked food, the pancreas will actually try to compensate digestive enzymes by enlarging. The white blood cells will also attempt to compensate by sharing their enzymes that were to be used in destroying bacteria and viruses. The immune system is therefore compromised.

What many do not realize is that enzymes can be depleted, and that in many people, they already are. In one study, the enzymes tested in 25 year-old subjects compared to 80 year-old subjects were markedly different. The younger group had thirty times more enzyme activity in their saliva.[43] Multiple enzyme deficiencies are extremely common in patients with allergies. On the other hand, food enzymes can be absorbed by the intestine and used at a later time.

Cooking food destroys all enzymes and some estimate that it may reduce up to 85% of nutrients. By not overeating, eating a predominance of raw foods and using supplemental digestive enzymes, one can increase the overall enzyme content in the body.

Unfortunately, the foods to which one is often allergic are foods that one may crave. These often are also the foods that are eaten most frequently. It is like an addiction. The food is craved and then eaten; the person feels better emotionally. Often, by just eliminating these allergenic foods, without any other change in habits or lifestyle, one may loose up to ten pounds.

The most common food allergies are dairy products, eggs, shellfish (crab, crayfish, lobsters, prawns, and shrimp), wheat (specifically the gluten in wheat, rye, and for some barley and oats), oranges, corn, strawberries, yeast, soy, beef, chocolate and tomatoes. Less common are peanuts and tree nuts.

One of the main food allergens is milk. Milk allergies, which are

extremely prevalent (60% of food sensitivities), have been shown to be associated with increased allergic reactions to goat's milk and beef. Sixty million North Americans are lactose intolerant (unable to digest the milk sugar in milk). Seventy percent of the world is lactase deficient, making them unable to digest the lactose in milk. In addition, allergies to soy products are noted in five to twenty percent of those with allergies to cow's milk. One could also be suffering from the penicillin in the milk. The time of year may further cloud the picture, since allergies to cow's milk become worse in the winter, and therefore an allergy may simply be thought of as a recurring cold.[44] Dairy food must be discarded when one is experiencing allergies, in addition to symptoms such as bedwetting, eczema, and colic, not to mention many respiratory ailments including ear infections, asthma and sinusitis. Remember to look for hidden forms of milk, often described as whey or casein.

Another major food allergen, corn, is associated with extremely unusual manifestations. Unfortunately this is a food that is found hidden in a variety of foods one would never expect. Being a thorough detective is a must.

Food intolerance symptoms may vary due to many factors. Let's take milk again for an example. How can one person who is lactose intolerant eat ice cream without difficulty but suffer abdominal cramping when they drink plain milk? The symptoms vary due to the amount of lactose in the dairy product. Chocolate milk is usually better tolerated than plain milk. Cheese and ice cream have less lactose and therefore fewer symptoms. Milk that is taken with meat has delayed emptying time and therefore fewer symptoms as the lactose (milk sugar) has more time to be digested. Yogurt (cultured milk) will also cause fewer symptoms, as the bacteria in the culture seem to survive the enzymes in the stomach and facilitate digestion in humans.[45] This variety of symptoms in the lactose intolerant person, as well as the ability to tolerate one form of the allergen and not another form, **does not** negate the negative, indirect influence to the immune system. The fact that the body occasionally will whisper to you that it is suffering by a painless passage of gas should not be any more ignored than if it yells at you by severe doubling over abdominal pain.

Children often develop allergies from foods being introduced too early for their digestive tract to digest them. Orange juice is probably the most allergenic for babies. It should not be given until the infant is at least one year old. Grains should not be introduced until the infant is drooling or teething. At that time the salivary glands are developed enough to produce the enzymes necessary for digesting these grains. Cooking grains for several hours will also improve digestibility. Cooking changes the  structure of the food and makes some foods less allergenic; this is particularly true for grains. Rice and oatmeal are great starter grains. Most are not allergic to rice. Pears and plums are a great first food for an infant. Ripe bananas since they are so versatile are also excellent. If a child does develop an allergy to a food, simply withhold it for three to four months, and substitute it with foods that may be tolerated.[46] Dr. A. Thrash recommends withholding peas and beans until the child is one year old and corn and tomatoes until two years old. Dry beans are more apt to cause symptoms than green beans or peas.[47]

Processed foods usually contain food additives or flavorings, foreign to the body. Genetic manipulation of plants has resulted in plants containing properties that can cross-react with normal tissues. The immune system was created to protect us from foreign substances. Allergies and degenerative diseases are often the result of a fatigued immune system. The defenses are now lowered from these alien substances.

Pesticides are also another factor in that, "two and a half billion pounds of **pesticides** are released into the environment each year. Sixty percent of these pesticides are used by farmers. Over 4,000 varieties of drugs are fed to animals which produce milk, eggs, and meat. About half of all the drugs manufactured in the United States are given to farm animals, many of them as medicated feed."[48]

Common offending **additives** include MSG (monosodium sodium glutamate), which is often hidden as hydrolyzed protein or natural flavoring. Dry roasted nuts and frozen vegetables and entrees often also contain MSG. Sulfites are another additive to be avoided. Sulfites are sprayed on fruits and vegetables at salad bars and dried fruit. They are found in seafood, fast food hamburgers, bottled lemon and lime juice, and frozen potatoes. They are also used as preservatives in many pharmaceuticals. The average person consumes an average of two to three mg. of sulfites per day. The average wine and beer drinker may average ten mg. a day. Those who frequent restaurants may reach one hundred and fifty mg. a day. Benzoates are another preservative that is found in fish and shrimp in extremely high levels. BHT/BHA are used in most packaged foods.[49, 50] Sodium nitrite and sodium nitrate are used in foods as preservatives (preventing bacterial growth) as well as to fix the color and improve the tastes of certain foods. This is predominantly found in cured meats, bacon, frankfurters, ham, sausages, and salmon. All of these additives tax the body unnecessarily and further stress the immune system. In addition, they may be a direct allergen.

An estimated five pounds a year of pesticides, flour "improvers", artificial colorings and preservatives, anti-staling compounds, etc., are ingested per person each year. Stop and think about that. More than six thousand new chemicals are tested in the United States each week![51] This is phenomenal! The body must deal with these toxins on a daily basis. Enzymes, vitamins and minerals are needed to neutralize these toxins. What happens as nutrients in the food decrease, while the chemicals on the food increase? It is only a matter of time before a malfunction will occur.

These additives further complicate the picture if attempts are made to determine allergens. For example, if there is suspicion of a wheat allergy, it is important to exclude all possible contaminates. These include the possible preservatives, the actual yeast in the wheat bread, or a contamination of yeast with corn, rye or barley. Pesticides on the wheat and the cornstarch on the container that it came in are other possible contaminates, thereby confusing the picture as to whether there is a true wheat allergy or a cross-contamination.

Even if the allergic food has been identified, a constant vigil may need to be maintained for hidden contamination. Examples of a hidden food may be a serving utensil used for several foods at a restaurant or the reuse of frying oil. A production plant that manufactures a certain food like peanut butter may not list peanuts as an ingredient even though peanut remnants may cross-contaminate other foods produced in the same plant. Many manufacturing plants use the same equipment in making ice cream, and dairy-free sorbet. The FDA only requires that an ingredient be listed if it comprises over 2% of the total ingredients. This is a problem, especially for a very reactive person.

A study from September1999 until March 2000 between federal and state investigators revealed that approximately 25% of companies manufactured foods with allergenic foods without listing them on their labels. It was also found that only half of these companies actually verified the accuracy of their labels.[52]

Depending on the health that is inherited, the lifestyle chosen, and the chemical exposure, there may or may not be the ability to metabolize toxins, foods, chemicals, or pollens as well as someone else. It may outwardly appear that the body, without difficulty, is handling these substances, but the cumulative affect on the body remains unknown. Unfortunately, there are few foods at the supermarket that have not been tampered with in some way.

Even **mercury fillings** may be a contributing factor to allergies. The mercury slowly seeps from the teeth while chewing. This is extremely

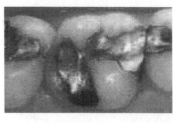 toxic to your immune system. In one study 90% of the patients patch tested for mercury were reactive. Mercury vapors have also been documented in the mouth after chewing or brushing. As long as these fillings remain, there are mercury vapors being breathed 365 days a year, 24 hours a day. This can overload the body and drain the immune system.

"Let us hear the conclusion of the whole matter..." Ecclesiastes 12:13.

Let it never be said, "I am only allergic to dust. No big deal." What MUST be remembered is that while dust may appear to be the cause of the runny nose, the body is attempting to communicate to us by this visible manifestation that it is not in optimal health. What is "put up with" or simply masked by medication now, WILL come back later in a future form. Eczema in a child may manifest as asthma in an adult. When ANY of the laws of health are violated, the immune system is weakened. The seeds that have often inadvertently been planted can easily yield an abundant harvest. Allergies are the result of a weakened immune system, an unhealthy bloodstream (from numerous toxins which have accumulated in the body), and an unfavorable internal and external environment. Following God's laws of health; however, contributes to a healthy blood stream and internal environment, and is thus favorable to a strong immune system.

Unfortunately, many lifestyle habits weaken the mucous membrane and the immune system, resulting in increased sensitivity to allergens. We will discuss many of these habits in the following section.

G.O.D.'S. P.L.A.N.

We will now begin to discuss what is often called the 8 laws of health. These laws are as important as the Ten Commandments. Recovery from any illness depends on many factors. These include thoughts and feelings, which affect our physical health directly, but also have a tremendous impact on our spiritual health. When the body is not performing at its peak condition, it is less receptive to the Holy Spirit's communication with us. We are going to utilize the acronym GOD'S PLAN to describe these laws as outlined below:

G= Godly Trust
O= Open Air
D = Daily Exercise
S = Sunshine
P = Plenty of Rest
L = Lots of Water
A = Always Temperate
N = Nutrition

Although your recovery depends on your lifestyle, let me encourage you with what has been said to be the 3 greatest letters in the English alphabet, N-O-W.[53] "Today if ye hear His voice, harden not your hearts." *Hebrews 3:15.* Forgiveness is given to all who desire, but one must first acknowledge the fact that in this area of your life, you have been deficient. Then ask for the strength to walk in these newly discovered paths. Do not procrastinate. Begin NOW. There is no time like the present.

GODLY TRUST

"Trust in the Lord with all thine heart, and lean not unto thine own understanding...It shall be health to thy navel and marrow to thy bones." *Proverbs 3:5, 8.*

It is amazing that it has taken science almost 2000 years to catch just a glimpse of the impact that the mind has on the body as discussed in the above text. The wise king Solomon expressed it repeatedly in many of the proverbs including the following: *"A merry heart doeth good like a medicine, but a broken spirit drieth the bones."* *Proverbs 17:22.* The ability to maintain a "trusting spirit" and a "merry heart" are vital to total wellness.

Endorphins are a class of hormones, which the body produces. Some of its effects are often compared to morphine, only to a greater degree. It can in some ways be called the "happy hormone." Endorphins positively impact the immune system, in addition to other things, in ways that scientists have still not completely determined. *"Whoso trusteth in the Lord, happy is he."* *Proverbs 16:20.* The happiness obtained by **Godly Trust** will automatically increase the level of endorphins.

When we are frustrated, worried, resentful, angry, or critical we are negatively impacting our immune system. Persistent indulgence in negative attitudes will affect the entire body directly and/or indirectly. Stress in any form will increase adrenaline levels. During periods of stress, digestion is incomplete. The undigested proteins and/or fats, which may result, form a type of alcohol in the blood. The circulation of the blood is diminished, acids accumulate in various muscles and the heart and arteries are damaged as cholesterol levels rise resulting in plaque deposits. Remember the key to good health is pure blood that is circulating freely. Negative attitudes prevent this from occurring. It has been reported "up to 85% of the thinking we regularly engage in is negative and self-defeating."[54]

Stress also affects mast cells. Remember, mast cells are the cells which release histamine, causing redness by vasodilatation and swelling due to an inflammatory process. There is an increase in both the number and their activation during times of stress.

The adrenal glands are important glands that produce more than thirty different steroids including cortisol, as well as some sex hormones, adrenaline and DHEA. During stress, the body manufactures additional amounts of adrenaline, an emergency alert hormone, and cortisol to combat potential emergencies. God made cortisol for periods of prolonged stress. These high cortisol levels, if sustained for long periods of time, will weaken the immune system. Chronic stress will eventually result in adrenal exhaustion, as the adrenal gland is required to continually produce excessive amounts of these hormones. The situation becomes almost cyclic in that the stress results in aggravated allergies and the allergies create stress in the body.[55]

All negative attitudes, which are a form of stress, deplete the cells of oxygen. These harmful thoughts and feelings may result in shallow chest breathing as well as diminish the free circulation of the blood. Oxygen is vital to optimal cell health.

Any stress, whether physical or mental, results in an additional expenditure of nutrients thus depleting the available supply. This loss of nutrients may contribute to allergic symptoms, as well as further stress the immune system. The body's ability to fight disease is diminished. All thoughts of fear, discontent, depression, guilt, anxiety, or remorse create an acidic condition in the body. Ideally the body maintains a slightly alkaline state.[57] When the body is acidic, there is a pre-disposition to a number of pathological conditions, including cancer. When we learn to replace those feelings with courage, contentment, cheerfulness, hope, love, praise and thankfulness, we will have won a major victory. *As Romans 12:21* reminds us, we must overcome evil with good. This prescription for overcoming is a daily decision.

The drying of the bones as described above in *Proverbs 17:22* comes as a result of a "broken spirit." It is in the bones that many of the white blood cells are produced. Remember that white blood cells are the body's "soldiers," and therefore, needed for optimum health. Anytime we allow ourselves to indulge in negative thinking or behavior we are limiting our immune system!

HOW TO APPLY:

What will increase the level of endorphins in our body? It is **Godly Trust**. The word trust is the same as faith. Fortunately, *"God hath dealt to every man the measure of faith." Romans 12:3.* This means we all have received a free gift of faith. The amount that we currently have is dependent on what was done with the initial gift of faith. Was it buried or cultivated?

Once you have begun following **GODS PLAN**, begin to mentally relax. Anxiety will block healing. Awareness of the environment and pollutants is inevitable, but worry is not. Practice **Godly Trust.**

To develop **Godly Trust** in our own lives, we must **first accept Jesus Christ as our personal Savior.** *"Come unto me all ye that labor and are heavy laden and I will give you rest." Matthew 11:28.* Our part is to come and acknowledge that we " *must be born again." John 3:7.* As we come acknowledging our sins, we ask for forgiveness for breaking God's laws of life. A sincere request is the only condition for the creation of a new heart. Christ freely forgives and empowers us with the Holy Spirit. It then becomes possible for us to live for Him. He will enable us by imparting wisdom and strength to live the healthy lives for which He has created us.

To continue to develop **Godly Trust** we are to **spend time daily in nature and in studying His Word,** so that we can personally determine His will for our lives. *"Stand still, and consider the wondrous works of God." Job 37:14.* It will quickly be discovered that nature is God's  second lesson book. We will learn that it is imperative for us to memorize the Bible that we may quickly recall key texts when needed. David wrote in Psalms, *"Thy word have I have I hid in my heart, that I might not sin against thee." Psalm 119:11.* The Bible is invaluable as a weapon. Jesus himself said, *"It is written"* when inundated with the attacks of the enemy, Satan. Read daily until you have memorized *Psalm 121* and *103* in the morning and *Psalm 91* and *23* before retiring.

The third step in developing **Godly Trust** is **prayer,** talking to God daily as to a friend. During times of prayer and meditation, take time periodically to ask yourself important questions such as, "What is my purpose in life? What road am I traveling and where will it end?" Prayerfully make a list of items that are reducing any aspect of health, be it physical, mental or spiritual, and ask your Father what can be done to alter or remove this influence.

When one develops **Godly Trust**, there will be no fear of the future. The relationship that has developed with our Creator and Sustainer has given a sense of peace. There is no need to dwell on past mistakes. Confidence is placed in a God who has an eagle's view. Earthly views are extremely limited — tunnel vision. God's eyes are all encompassing knowing the beginning as well as the end.

Prayer is essential to healing. As our friendship with our Savior deepens we will **trust** Him enough to say, *"not my will but thine be done." Matthew 6:10.* When we do this we again are following Jesus' example. This intimate relationship that we have developed with the Great Physician allows us to understand that no matter what happens on this earth, there is an eternity awaiting us in the new earth, if we are faithful.

The last step in this walk of faith is **telling others what wonderful things God is doing for us.** Witnessing to others is vital, for while it encourages others, it also brings us closer to God. This should be done daily in our homes as we worship together in the morning and evening. As the opportunity unfolds, share with those brought in our pathway. Begin sharing with others your appreciation for them.

"Let us hear the conclusion of the whole matter…"
Ecclesiastes 12:13.

Godly Trust is faith. **Godly Trust** has a direct effect on our endorphin levels, which affects our immune system. A lack of **Godly Trust** results in stress. Negative attitudes and stress inhibit digestion and circulation, resulting in an acidic condition in the body. The faith that God has given us may be increased by daily asking God to  recreate in us a new heart, spending time in the Bible and nature, and staying in an attitude of prayer and submission. Daily memorize the Word. Developing the habit of daily counting your blessings and sharing them with others is invaluable. Have faith in God.

> *"Without faith (Godly Trust) it is impossible to please Him."*
> *Hebrews 11:6.*

OPEN AIR

"And God said, Let there be a firmament in the midst of the waters; and let it divide the waters from the waters." **Genesis 1:6.**

Three thousand gallons of air move through our respiratory tract every day. This air is filled with life-giving oxygen that is necessary for optimal cell health. **Open Air** carries an electrical charge that is referred to as negative or positive ions. The more

negative ions there are in the air, the more beneficial is the air. Negative ions assist the immune system in its destruction of bacteria and germs. They cause one to feel refreshed and exhilarated, as often occurs after a walk in the woods, a thunderstorm or upon visiting a waterfall. Unfortunately when fresh air enters our home,adheres to the walls and furniture, loosing its negative charge. Therefore, a constant flow of fresh air is needed.

Although the major component of air is not oxygen, it is available in the right proportion for our needs. Oxygen is crucial for cell health. Negative ions may impact oxygen availability by increasing the affinity of hemoglobin and oxygen. Hemoglobin is the portion of the red blood cell that carries the oxygen. Total lung capacity is improved by negative ions[57] as well as air quality. Dust (up to 45%), bacteria (up to 95%) and smoke levels in the air have all been found to be lower in air with high amounts of negative ions.[58] These ions are also linked to serotonin levels,[59] affecting mood, digestion, blood pressure and heart rate. Excessive positive ions may result in excess serotonin, which could cause severe headaches[60] and other symptoms associated with decreased oxygen for the cells.

The jury is still out on all of the benefits of negative ions, but research has shown many positive effects. Decreasing pain levels post-operatively, as well as activating cilia (microscopic hair like filaments in the respiratory tract) after their movement had decreased due to tobacco inhalation, are a few of the positive effects.

Optimum fresh **Open Air** is available by simply going outside and breathing. Although this seems simple enough, it often requires retraining. Most of us are shallow and irregular breathers. Optimal exchange of oxygen and carbon dioxide occurs with deep breathing, which is natural for babies. Observe a baby or a child asleep. With advancing age, the natural God-given ability to breathe properly is lost. With proper deep breathing, the stomach moves out while inhaling and returns to its prior resting position when exhaling. On the other hand, many of us utilize only the upper portion of our lungs allowing waste to accumulate in the lower region of the lungs. This is noted by observing the chest wall moving out with inhaling instead of the abdomen.What are we breathing anyway? Is there really such a thing as fresh air? Despite the fact that outdoor air is often contaminated with smog, exhaust and chemicals from manufacturing plants and agriculture, indoor air is often more polluted than outdoor air; some estimate that it may be up to 100% more polluted.[61] Since 90% of the average American's time is often spent indoors, it is therefore important to reduce indoor air pollution.

One of the greatest sources of indoor air pollution is carpet. The fibers in the carpet trap and retain dust, pollen and other microorganisms. Other indoor pollutants are dust mites, cockroach parts, formaldehyde, pet danders, hair, mold spores, carbon tetrachloride, chloroform, chemical gases, tobacco smoke, and benzene. As most buildings are tightly sealed, these pollutants are trapped and re-circulated resulting in "sick buildings".

Newer, airtight homes are often tightly sealed and dry. This dryness will impact the mucus membranes in the respiratory tract as well as impair the movement of cilia. Cilia, remember, are the microscopic hair like

filaments that line the respiratory tract. They wave back and forth to remove fine, foreign inhaled particles that become trapped on the healthy hydrated mucous layer, which lines the respiratory tract. This mucous layer also contains important substances needed to bind with foreign particles. Normally this mucous is cleared six times in one hour by coughing or swallowing. If the air is too dry, the dehydrated mucous cannot trap the foreign dust particles. The cilia also will not move as well, therefore, the contaminant particles enter into the lungs.

HOW TO APPLY:

Several times a day, particularly when stressed, pay attention to your breathing. Deep breathing does take practice. It may seem so elementary, but it is vital! This is the best way to open the tiny air sacs in the lungs that are called alveoli, for optimal exchange of the beneficial oxygen with wastes. **To practice deep breathing, go outside in the fresh air, place a hand on your abdomen and take a deep breath in through the nose. Hold it to the slow count of ten or twenty, and then exhale slowly through the mouth. Take longer to exhale then inhale to ensure that all of the possible residual air in the lungs is exhaled. Feel your abdomen contract with the full release of air. Wait ten seconds before repeating. Initially do this ten times, increasing to twenty times, a minimum of three times a day.** With acute illness, particularly respiratory illness, increase to hourly repetitions while awake. Do not be discouraged if this seems difficult at first. With persistence this will become natural. Wear loose clothing so that the abdomen may move freely and avoid belts. Clothing should ideally hang from the shoulders instead of the waist. Men should wear suspenders instead of belts.

Make it a habit to spend time outside everyday, despite the weather. Although we cannot be in the **Open Air** all of the time, we can allow fresh air into our homes and work places. This is particularly important for sleeping rooms. Do not sleep under a draft, but keep some windows open to allow ventilation, and these ideally should not be directly across from each other.

Vacuum all carpets at least weekly. To keep a carpet clean one needs a HEPA– type filter (high-efficiency particulate arrestor) or water capture system. A less expensive alternative may be Dupont's *Hysurf* vacuum cleaner bags, which seem to have the efficacy of expensive "allergy" vacuum cleaners.[62] Of course, another alternative is to simply remove all carpets so that floors may be swept and mopped on a regular basis or to purchase one of the few 100% wool carpets, made without chemical or synthetic materials.

Other clean carpet tips include taking your shoes off outside or purchasing short fiber carpets for easier cleaning. One may look under the carpet for any signs of stains, rusty nails or mold. Mold should be cleaned with a 10% bleach water solution. NEVER put carpet in your bathroom.

Having carpets professionally cleaned often results in worsening of symptoms due to the cleaning agent. If carpet must be cleaned, use a non-scented, emulsifying, cleaning agent that has no ammonia, alcohol or petroleum products, and that has no suds. Ensure that there are no damp areas left, as that will feed mold and bacteria.

There are many ways to improve your inside air quality. Indoor plants can effectively reduce air pollution, in particular the spider plant, aloe vera, ficus, English ivy, chrysanthemums and Boston ferns. Some have estimated that two plants minimum per one hundred square feet of floor space will help to improve air quality by filtering humidifying, and oxygenating the air.

Air humidity should be maintained at approximately 40%. Air humidity is extremely important in the winter when heating units increase the dryness of the air. A pan of water near the heating duct or a wet towel hung in a bedroom is often sufficient to increase humidity. The new small fountains that are available are another option. They do need to be kept running constantly though, so that bacteria and/or mold will not grow in the unit. If you do opt for a humidifier, warm-mist humidifiers are superior to cool-mist and steam-mist units although, they may use more electricity. Cool-mist units emit a fine mineral dust unless used with distilled water and steam-mist units become very hot. Depending on how safety-conscious the persons involved are, this obviously could be dangerous. Empty the humidifier every morning and allow it to dry out to reduce the chance of mold production.

An optional air purification unit should provide air similar to that found after a thunderstorm. They should produce ions and ozone, which will cover varying amounts of square feet. These reduce odors, pollutants and other particles in the air. The negative ions in fresh air or those produced

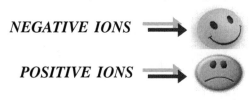

NEGATIVE IONS

POSITIVE IONS

by the air filtration device will "nab" some of the potential allergens. As they fall to the floor, they may be vacuumed. Dusting with a wet cloth will further reduce the dust. The *Dupont Wizard* dust cloth is another option.

Depending on where you live, having your windows open may be sufficient. Despite the weather, keep windows open to some degree year round, provided the outdoor air does not contain heavier contaminates than the air inside. If you do live in an area where you are periodically warned to stay indoors due to outdoor contaminants, still have some fresh air from outside, indoor plants are a must and an additional air filter may be necessary.

Remember furnace filters need to be replaced regularly. Write a reminder on your calendar if necessary. Go to a hardware store for a 3M-pleated filter under the names of Filtret and Electret. These are much more effective than those found in supermarkets. Air duct cleaning should also be considered, as filtering cannot remove all particles. In addition once the air is filtered, it still has to travel through the duct. Keep your thermostat between 65 and 70 degrees. Do not smoke or allow anyone else to smoke in your home and/or work area. Avoid secondhand smoke at all costs. Keep pets outside.

Use natural fibers as often as possible for clothing and in the home. Limit exposure to toxic cleaning substances. There are many nontoxic-cleaning solutions available.

If there is a need for additional aid in improving the indoor air quality, begin with a negative ion generator in your bedroom, placed two feet from a wall. If money allows, an additional one in your workplace would be the second recommendation. Make sure that the ionizer does not produce excessive negative ions. Reportedly the *Sinus Survival Air Vitalizer* by Air Tech International is a much more economical option. This not only cleans the air but also maintains negative ions.[63]

"Let us hear the conclusion of the whole matter..."

Ecclesiastes 12:13.

Open Air purifies the blood and provides the cells with oxygen. This is vital for healthy cells. **Open Air** provides negative ions, which strengthen the immune system, improves our mental attitude as well as increases oxygen availability and overall air quality. Spend time daily outdoors and always provide some fresh air in your home by way of plants and open windows. Avoid as many chemicals as possible. Practice deep breathing exercises regularly. Monitor your breathing habits especially during times of stress.

"He giveth to all life, and breath, and all things." Acts 17:25.

DAILY EXERCISE

"And the Lord God took the man, and put him into the garden of Eden to dress it and to keep it...In the sweat of thy face shalt thou eat bread, till thou return unto the ground." **Genesis 2:15, 3:19.**

Oxygen is vital to the health of the body. When we **Exercise**, the oxygen demand of the body is increased. Although the muscles receive the majority of this oxygen, the remainders of the cells in the body are also oxygenated. Airflow through the nose is increased with **Exercise**. Oxygen creates an environment, which is particularly beneficial to the respiratory system.

During **Exercise,** the cells of the body are allowed to unload their waste into the blood. The waste is then discarded by one of the eliminative organs, such as the skin or lungs, rather than remaining in the cells as a stagnant pool. Have you noticed the healthy glow one has after exercising? All of the eliminative organs receive increased blood flow during **Exercise**, which aids in elimination.

The lymphatic system which includes lymph fluid, ducts, nodes and vessels, is responsible for removing cellular wastes and foreign particles located between the actual cells. This draining system has no pump of its own and is dependent upon the movement of muscles to move its fluid.

Exercise is also extremely beneficial for stress. There are substances called endorphins that are released during **Exercise,** which aid in general outlook as well as the ability to handle stress. The sleep is sweet and the body more relaxed after a day that includes **Exercise**. *The sleep of a labouring man is sweet." Ecclesiastes 5:12.* Energy is restored by **Exercise** and the bones are strengthened. Digestion is improved. The numbers of blood vessels in the body increase in number and size thereby increasing the availability of oxygen. The lungs also become more efficient.

HOW TO APPLY:
Find a form of **Exercise** that you enjoy and indulge yourself. Walk on a regular basis. Start a garden, do some stretches. Aerobic **Exercise** is

needed on a regular basis but remember that a gentle stretching program accompanied with deep breathing is also very important. There is no time like the present to start. 30 minutes a day is the minimum, but of course start gradually. One does not have to become a marathon runner. Many studies have reported the injurious results of strenuous **Exercise** over a prolonged period of time. Simply schedule a walking time every day. Gradually increase the pace, and always begin and end with a stretch. Do not walk at a pace in which conversation becomes difficult. If you develop chest pain while exercising, stop! Short walks, carrying groceries, and climbing a flight of stairs versus taking the elevator may be incorporated into one's daily routine. Leisure walking is beneficial after a meal to aid digestion; but plan strenuous **Exercise** either thirty minutes prior or two hours after the meal, so that there is no interference with digestion.

Gardening is another form of **Exercise,** which is God given. *Jeremiah 29:5* instructs us "… and plant gardens and eat the fruit of them." The first gardener was Adam and the rewards of a manicured yard or homegrown produce will add more joy to your **Exercise.** All useful, manual labor or **Exercise** results in a two-fold benefit.

Another favorable form of **Exercise** is the rebounder. This form of **Exercise** is particularly beneficial to the lymphatic fluid in the lymph vessels. 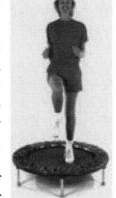 It also benefits the joints, as they will not receive the impact that would occur if the feet were landing on a hard surface. Be creative when rebounding and use it outdoors as much as possible. If one is unable to rebound, just sitting on a rebounder (or putting your feet on the rebounder) while someone else is jumping, is a passive way to still benefit the lymphatic system.

For those who are unable to perform any form of **Exercise**, massage is vital. This passive form of **Exercise** will also increase circulation, the function of the immune system and improve waste removal.

Early morning is the best time to **Exercise**, particularly in the summer. In the winter, the cold night air may trap carbon monoxide, sulfur dioxide and nitrogen dioxide. Therefore, it is best, if you live in an urban area, to **Exercise** during the winter months in the evening. Avoid mouth breathing during exercise as the body's natural filtration system, the nose and sinuses, are bypassed.

If you suffer from nasal congestion, it is recommended that after completing your **Exercise** regime, including the cool down, that you have 5-10 minutes of moist steam. This will increase mucous flow and expectoration. Although steam inhalers are now readily available at most drug stores, sitting under a towel that is draped over a pot of boiling water is a simple alternative, as is stepping into a bathroom filled with shower steam.

"Let us hear the conclusion of the whole matter…"
Ecclesiastes 12:13.

Daily exercise increases the availability of oxygen to the cells of the body. The circulation of the blood and waste removal from the cell is increased during **Exercise**. The lymphatic fluid is also activated. Stress is reduced by **Daily Exercise. Exercise should be enjoyed and partaken of daily.**

"The labour of the righteous tendeth to life." Proverbs 10:16.

SUNSHINE

"...for he maketh his sun to rise on the evil, and on the good..."
Matthew 5:45.

The sun has amazing, God-given, healing power. It energizes the body. It is an efficient germ killer. The sun's rays should always be welcome in your home as a free disinfectant. It will reduce molds and bacteria. **Sunlight** will increase the amount of oxygen that the red blood cells can carry in the blood, as well as improve the circulation of blood. **Sunlight**  increases the use of oxygen in the tissues. This oxygen is what is needed for optimum cell function.

The numbers of white blood cells are also increased by **Sunlight**. These cells are the fighting soldiers in the body, which are necessary for an optimum functioning immune system. Lymphocytes are one of the white blood cells that fight disease in the bloodstream by identifying germs and foreign substances and then producing antibodies to fight them. They are increased for up to three weeks after sun exposure. This enhances your ability to fight infection and decreases the reproduction of viruses. Other white blood cells, called neutrophils have been found to double their rate of engulfing bacteria after sun exposure.

Sunlight positively stimulates many of the glands of the body, including the adrenal, pineal and thyroid. The pineal gland produces melatonin, which regulates the body's internal clock, protects the body from free radical damage, as well as strengthens the immune system. **Sunlight,** striking the skin provides vitamin D for the body.

Sunlight stimulates liver function. The liver filters the blood from harmful substances. All antigens and allergens eventually end up in the liver to be removed from the body by the stool or urine. Many steps occur in the liver for this to occur therefore a healthy liver is vital for proper detoxification.

Sunlight also increases the negatively charged ions in the air that we breathe. This brings marked relief for hay fever sufferers. Most heating and cooling systems remove this beneficial negative charge from the air. By opening your windows or being outside as much as possible you will receive the optimum ratio of negative to positive ions, as God intended.

HOW TO APPLY:

To sunbathe, **start gradually**. Ideally, if a private space is available, the whole body should be exposed starting with five minutes a day. Exposing the sun to only your face and hands, beginning with ten to fifteen minutes a day is also beneficial. Increase this time by five-minute increments. The goal is thirty to forty-five minutes a day for each side of your body. The amount of time that you spend will need to depend upon your skin color. A darker skinned person, due to their increased melanin, may start with fifteen minutes a day and increase with fifteen-minute increments instead of five minutes.[64] Sunbathing should not be done when the sun is at its peak. During the winter, sunbathing should be done during the noon hours. In the summer, it is best to sunbathe before 11 AM or after 4 PM.

Avoiding free fat intake will reduce cancer risk. This includes oils, margarines and all dairy and meat products. DO NOT GET SUNBURNED! The skin should never turn red. If you choose to sunbathe with clothes on, use loosely woven white material. If a private area is accessible then gradually begin sunbathing your liver and your lower back and spine. Sunscreens are not necessary, just clean skin.[65]

Open the drapes and windows whenever possible so that the **Sunlight** may enter your home.

"Let us hear the conclusion of the whole matter…"
Ecclesiastes 12:13.

Sunlight will increase the circulation in the body and the oxygen supply, as well as positively affect the white blood cells. **Sunlight** affects many of the glands and hormones of the body. **Sunlight** also stimulates the liver so that allergens and toxins may be excreted. Sun exposure should be obtained daily.

"But unto them that fear my name shall the Sun of righteousness arise with healing in His wings." Malachi 4:2.

PROPER REST

"...yea, thou shalt lie down, and thy sleep shall be sweet."
Proverbs 3:24.

In this fast paced society, it is easy to forget that rest is one of the most overlooked and cheapest methods to strengthen the immune system. The average American suffers from sleep deprivation, which diminishes immunity. We are all guilty of attempting to crowd more activities into a day, and subsequently the night, than can be accomplished. Turning the night into day is a fatal act. *"It is vain for you to rise up early, to sit up late, to eat the bread of sorrows; for so He giveth His beloved sleep." Psalm 127:2.*

All of the cells in the body rest at some point. Many vital functions occur during this time. When we rest at night, many hormones needed for growth, repair, disposition and immune function are produced. The brain is actually very active while we sleep. Adequate hydration during the day will aid in its proper function at night. Irritability, anxiety, depression, and lethargy are all associated with inadequate sleep.

HOW TO APPLY:

Have a regular rising and bedtime every day. The body functions best on rhythms. It is therefore imperative that one arises and retires at a set time. Regularity is vital. **The sleep obtained prior to midnight is twice as beneficial as sleep after midnight; therefore 9:30 P.M. should be the latest that one goes to bed.** Your body will learn to relish this time to rebuild and revitalize.

Equally important, if not even more important is rising at the appointed time. "Sleeping in" is a quick way to develop jet lag. If you are still tired after rising, then add a nap before lunch, but **do not sleep in.** This early morning rising is your time to talk with your Creator, and is important in resetting your biological clock to its new schedule.

If anxious and suffering from insomnia, do not despair. *"I will lay me down in peace, and sleep: for thou, Lord, only makest me dwell in safety."*

Psalm 4:8. Claim the promises. Potential stimulation such as problem solving, caffeine, television, computers, noise, etc., is to be avoided. Supper, if eaten at all, should be extremely light, something that would digest quickly such as fruit alone or fruit with zwieback. Warm tub soaks prior to bed with slow, deep breathing exercises are also beneficial. You may find chamomile, hops, skullcap, valerian or passionflower teas helpful. These teas do not alter your quality of sleep, as most sleeping pills will. Celery juice is another alternative. Take distracting items out of the bedroom. This includes exercise equipment, computers, and ironing boards. Establish a bedtime ritual and this will soon become habit. **Most of all, let the last thought at night and the first thought in the morning be of our wonderful Sustainer, the Creator.**

"Come ye yourselves apart ...and rest awhile." Mark 6:31. Periodically allocate time for a simple change. Find a new hobby, enjoy a concert, go berry picking, play with the neighborhood children, visit a nursing home or go on a picnic by a waterfall. These forms of relaxation can give your week a needed boost.

Do not forget the importance of the weekly rest, or the Sabbath. This time of rejuvenation is essential for physical, mental, and spiritual wholeness. It is interesting that in Biblical times the penalty for breaking the Sabbath was death by stoning. The penalty has not changed. True, one may not be literally stoned to death, but there is a slow and steady impact on your body that results in death by our not taking the 7th day as a day of rest and meditation, praise and fellowship as our Creator intended.

"Let us hear the conclusion of the whole matter..."
Ecclesiastes 2:13.

During sleep, the cells in the body are repaired and rebuilt. Our immune systems cannot perform at peak levels when the cells are fatigued. Establish a regular bedtime as well as a bedtime ritual. Take time for rest during the week in addition to your regular sleep time. Keep the Sabbath as outlined in our Owners Manual, the Bible. See *Exodus 20:8-11.*

"There remaineth therefore a rest to the people of God."
Hebrews :9.

LOTS OF WATER

"...and let them give us pulse to eat, and water to drink."
Daniel 1:12.

Our bodies are composed of approximately 60-70% **Water.** The brain and blood contain approximately 75% **water.** Adequate **water** intake is essential for proper cell function. Blood volume will reach an optimum level with proper **water** intake; this increases oxygen available to  the cells. With this increased circulation, the colon, kidneys, skin and lungs can remove the cell waste in a more efficient manner.

Adequate **water** is necessary for lubrication of the mucous membranes that line the respiratory tract. Secretions are thinned allowing ease with expectoration. The sinuses will drain much more effectively when one is well hydrated. Mucous membranes will also be able to have increased resistance to infection.

HOW TO APPLY:
A basic guide to water intake is ½ of your weight in ounces. If a person weighs 160 lbs., they need to drink eighty ounces of water a day. This would be ten 8oz. glasses of water. Spread this out throughout the day, between meals. If a person has increased perspiration, they, of course would need to increase their water intake. If the urine is not pale, the **water** intake needs to be increased. **Establish the habit of carrying water with you wherever you go.** Many wait until they are thirsty to drink. Unfortunately, at that point they are already dehydrated. Cultivate the habit of indulging in this elixir throughout the day.

From 30 minutes to 1 hour before a meal, until 1-2 hours after each meal, drinking water should be avoided. Also do not drink water that is too hot or too cold. The body must adjust the temperature of the **Water** in the stomach before it can be utilized; this is a waste of energy.

Drinking water does not mean drinking sodas, juice or tea for your water supply. **water** means **water. A great way to start your day is**

with two glasses of pure room temperature water. Add half of the juice of a lemon in each glass.

Always run the **Water** from your tap before using if it has been sitting in the pipes for a few hours. Do not drink **water** from hot **water** pipes, as hot **water** may contain higher levels of lead and other metals. **AVOID water that has been treated with chlorine and/or fluoride.** But remember that if this is all that is available, it is more beneficial than no **water** at all. If there are concerns regarding the safety of *your* tap water, adding a blade of wheat grass to a glass of tap water will help purify it. Call your local health department to have your tap **water** tested. Bottled **water** is not always what you think it is. A **water** filter system may need to be considered if your tap **Water** is not suitable. If you choose to drink distilled **water**, add trace minerals regularly.

A **warm bath** is another wonderful treat. Evening showers or baths

are essential during the pollen season. **Alternating hot & cold water showers** are therapeutic and stimulating to the system. You will find it to be an excellent way to jumpstart your day. Begin with water as warm as you can tolerate. Continue with the warm water for approximately three to five minutes then rapidly change the temperature to cold water to the face, mid chest and spine for one minute and then return to warm/hot water. Continue alternating at least three times and end with cold. A **cool bath** is another option that is beneficial upon arising in the morning. This should be followed by a dry brush or rough washcloth rub.

For nasal congestion, simply putting the feet in hot water, increasing the temperature as tolerated for approximately 20-30 minutes is beneficial. The treatment is ended with ice water poured over the feet, which are then dried thoroughly, followed by a period of rest. Hot footbaths should not be done on a diabetic or someone with impaired sensation of the extremities. Cold compresses to the head simultaneously will aid in decreasing the congestion.

Alternating hot and cold compresses to the sinus region for congestion can be done in a similar manner as the alternating hot and cold shower but they should be preceded by a warm footbath. Alternating hot and cold to the sinus region should be done three times a day initially, and then may be reduced as symptoms decrease.

A **humidifier or vaporizer** may be used in the winter to increase the room humidity. **Cold compresses** may be applied to the eyes if they are irritated.

Steam treatments may be obtained by stepping into a steamed bathroom that has been heated by the shower, by placing one's face over a pot of steaming water or by tabletop vaporizers that are now readily available. Eucalyptus or tea tree oil may be added to the water. Steam should be used two to four times a day during an acute infection or as needed. Steam may also be used to re-hydrate the mucous membranes that have come in contact with dirty or dry air. Make a conscious effort to breathe through your nose.

Nasal irrigation should be used daily two to four times a day **after each steam treatment**. Moisture aids the nasal passages in restoring normal cilia function. Their movement is limited by mucous as well as bacteria, dust particles and many other substances found in smoke. Prepare the irrigating solution daily:

1 cup of bottled or boiled and then cooled (lukewarm) water

1/3 tsp of non-iodized table salt

A tiny pinch of baking soda

Plain water is usually irritating, thus, the baking soda and salt will make the solution similar to normal body fluid.

For small children, one may irrigate with 10-20 drops of the solution in each nostril with an eyedropper. An ear syringe may also be used, as well as a water pik with a nasal irrigator attachment set to the lowest possible pressure. For adults and older children use ½ cup for each nostril. During irrigation, remember to keep your mouth open, while keeping your mouth open, breathe through your nose. This irrigation may be done with a **neti pot**, a porcelain pot that is gentle, convenient and available at M.E.E.T. Ministry and most health food stores.

The bathing of the membranes with salt water keeps them moist and eliminates pollutants and particles that the cilia normally remove. Although this may be considered temporary, it does supply long-term benefits by helping the mucous membranes heal.

"Let us hear the conclusion of the whole matter…"
Ecclesiastes 12:13.

The body is 60-70% **water**. When we have inadequate **water** intake, the circulation in the body, as well as the removal of waste from the body, is impacted. **water** increases the oxygen content of the cells. **water** should be used externally in a variety of forms to increase circulation and enhance cleansing of the body.

"As the hart panteth after the water brooks, so panteth my soul after thee, O God." Psalm 42:1.

ALWAYS TEMPERATE

"And every man that striveth for the mastery is temperate in all things." **1 Corinthians 9:25.**

The word **Temperance** embraces two important principles. The first is to abstain from any harmful substance. This includes all alcohol, narcotics, caffeine, and tobacco. Substances that contain vinegar, irritating spices and sugar should also be avoided. The second principle is to exercise moderation in all things that are beneficial. One needs to eat, but overeating results in the formation of alcohol that is detrimental to not only the liver but also to every cell in the body. *"Blessed art thou oh land when thy...princes eat in due season for strength and not for drunkenness." Ecclesiastes 10:17.* Exercise is also important but when we exercise to extreme, lactic acid accumulates in the body until there is adequate oxygen for its removal.

Temperance covers every area that has been discussed in this book. As we have learned and applied the sundry principles, and begin practicing them in moderation, we are exercising **Temperance**. **Temperance** applies to all of the health issues, be it sunbathing, exercise, drinking, eating or rest.

One area of **Temperance** that is often overlooked is dress. Popular fashion unfortunately dictates many of our habits. These are often violating the law of **Temperance**. The manner in which we dress affects the circulation of the body, particularly the limbs. When clothes are worn which leave the arms and legs exposed to the cold, there is an imbalance in the circulation; the blood is pooled in the trunk of the body. Covering the limbs adequately will ensure proper circulation of the blood and decrease potential congestion. This is important for the immune system to function properly and for oxygenation of the cells. Should congestion occur, there is an increased risk of disease. These include conditions involving the pulmonary and reproductive organs.

Another often unmentioned area of **Temperance** is balance in sexual activity with our spouses. God has ordained sex between spouses, but over stimulation of the sexual organs results in the loss of important minerals and vitamins. Moderation must be practiced in all things.

Abstaining from all harmful substances includes sugar. Sugar is a poison that wreaks havoc on the immune system. It  depletes the body of essential B vitamins, which are necessary in maintaining a healthy nervous and therefore, stress-resistant system. Sugar, an extremely moldy food, also taxes the adrenal glands as well as the pancreas. It contributes to an acidic condition of the body. One teaspoon of sugar zaps white blood cells for up to six hours. Amazingly, just two cans of soda can result in a 92% drop in the phagocytes' ability to engulf antigens for as much as five hours.[66] This also occurs by drinking a typical milkshake. The 92% decrease in phagocytosis results in a white blood cell ingesting only one bacterium in a twelve hour period, quite a contrast to the norm. Disease may easily gain the upper hand in a sugar filled diet. It has been estimated that the average American consumes approximately 150 pounds of sugar per year, much of which is hidden.

Caffeine is another poison whose severity is often not understood. Found in coffee, teas, sodas and chocolate, caffeine unnaturally stimulates the body. It produces an effect similar to stress causing an increase in "stress" hormones. It delays the digestion of food, as well as increases the amount of acid that the stomach produces. The result is often heartburn as well as ulcers. Caffeine is associated with an increased risk for a number of cancers, as well as depression or anxiety, miscarriages, osteoporosis, birth defects, dehydration and heart palpitations.

Alcohol, tobacco and drugs will not be discussed, as there is an abundance of information on their detrimental effects on the brain, liver, kidneys, and lungs. With the indulgence of these substances, the eliminative organs are not able to concentrate on assisting the body in the removal of allergens. They are fighting a battle to maintain their normal function while removing these toxic substances. God has never intended for the bodies to be contaminated with such.

Temperance can only be exercised through the power of the Holy Spirit. We may make vows and promises, but unless we have Christ to empower us, these promises are just like ropes of sand.

"Let us hear the conclusion of the whole matter..."
Ecclesiastes 12:13.

Temperance is self-control. This can only be obtained through Christ Jesus. Remember, all things that are beneficial are to be done in **moderation** and ALL harmful substances are to be eliminated. Intemperance increases the amount of toxins in the body, which are injurious to the immune system as well as all of the eliminative organs.

"Now unto him that is able to keep you from falling..." Jude 24.

NUTRITION

"...feed me with food convenient for me." Proverbs 30:6.

As previously stated, the key to a healthy body is pure blood flowing freely to all of the cells in the body, providing the needed oxygen and nutrients while removing any cellular waste. The vitamins, minerals and other nutrients obtained in our food provide the building  blocks to maintain a healthy, disease-fighting body.

The original diet outlined by our Creator in Genesis informs us that fruit, nuts, grains and vegetables are to be freely enjoyed. This diet is the diet that we will enjoy in the new earth. By giving the **G.L.A.D.** (God's Life-Activating Diet) a chance for only ten days, one will quickly realize its advantages over the **S.A.D.** (Standard American Diet). The **"GLAD"** diet is high in fiber and nutrients, low in protein and fats. The **"SAD"** diet is high in protein and fats, which stress the liver and kidneys. There is also a lack of fiber resulting in constipation as well as increased cholesterol. This further decreases the purity of the blood in the system as well as its circulation. Nutrients that feed the cells are also very limited on the **"SAD"** diet.

The **"GLAD"** diet will freely use whole grains, which contain all of the needed B vitamins to maintain a healthy system. It will regularly include green vegetables, which contain chlorophyll and calcium, as well as the colorful vegetables for their various phytochemicals. Fruits are necessary for cleansing. Fruits and vegetables both aid in alkalinizing the body. On the other hand, animal products are extremely acidic, high in protein and fat and lack fiber. They often contain high amounts of bacteria. Hormones are regularly injected in animals that are to be sold, to increase their size and thus the price obtained from the consumer. These hormones cause abnormal cell reproduction. Processed meats, which are sold in stores and restaurants, contain high amounts of chemicals, including sodium nitrate.

Many express concern regarding adequate protein on a vegetarian diet. This concern is unnecessary. As long as one is eating a variety of foods and obtaining adequate calories, there will be adequate protein. The following advice may seem restrictive initially, but *Job 23:12* states, *"I have esteemed the words of his mouth more than my necessary food."* Learning to place God's will as outlined in **GOD'S PLAN** as a primary goal in your life will aid you in developing new taste buds and habits.

Other nutritional tips that will aid in our quest for following God's Plan are to eat a **variety** of foods. Many eat the same foods in a different form everyday. Eating a variety of raw, juiced, or steamed fruits and vegetables is inestimable. Organic, locally grown, non-irradiated produce should be eaten as much as possible. Make sure the fruit is tree or vine ripened, if possible. Eat fruit and vegetables in their season. Undigested food, and fat in particular, contributes to mucous production and fried foods are extremely difficult to digest. The fleeting enjoyment is not worth the price. Avoid all foods that contain artificial colorings. Salt is to be used sparingly. There are many possible substitutes including dulse or kelp. Read labels carefully. Do not use aluminum cookware. Aluminum has been associated with poor calcium metabolism, forgetfulness, decreased liver and kidney function, anemia, nervousness, colic and many gastrointestinal disturbances. There is also a link with Alzheimer's.

Only eat when relaxed and truly able to enjoy the meal. Prior to

eating make time to take a few deep breaths to relax, and take a moment to express gratitude. Do not eat standing up and chew each mouthful at least thirty times. If you have digestive problems you may need to double that to sixty times. Chew your liquids and drink your food. Always leave the table feeling that

you could eat a little more. Space your meals five to six hours apart. Most will find that two meals a day are sufficient. A third meal if eaten, should be extremely light. Do not skip breakfast. Nothing is to be eaten when experiencing negative emotions or at night prior to retiring.

Try to **eat at least 70% of your food raw, and 30% cooked**. Increasing the percentage of raw food, particularly for someone that is older or who has previously not enjoyed and profited from a healthy diet, would also be beneficial. Remember, cooked food has no digestive enzymes, thus requiring the body to supplement enzymes for adequate digestion of food. Your digestive system may temporarily need extra support in the form of digestive enzymes from years of stress and/or abuse. Read all labels to ensure that you are obtaining the enzyme from a non-animal source. Digestive enzymes may be obtained at most health food stores. All possible causes of food allergies will need correction. These may include inadequate hydrochloric acid in the stomach, inadequate pancreatic enzymes, bowel toxicity or bacterial imbalance including a candida infection.

Avoid the common trigger foods for allergies until it is determined that you are not allergic to them. They may be resumed in your diet in about two months, usually without difficulty.[67]

There is a simple pulse test for food allergies that was developed by Dr. Coca. This consists of taking a resting pulse rate for one minute before rising and thirty minutes before a meal. After eating the food you are testing, re-check the pulse. This should be done at thirty and sixty minutes after eating the food. If the pulse rate increases more than twelve beats per minute, that food should be removed from the diet for at least one month. It can then be retested. While this is a useful test, all foods will not affect the pulse.[68]

Another simple way to test for a potential allergy is to avoid the suspected foods for four to seven days. Then challenge the body with a meal of just that single item in a pesticide free form. If any pains, rashes, mental fogginess, fatigue, etc., occur, one may suspect a possible allergy. Remember, foods that are eaten on a regular basis or that are often craved are frequently indicative of an allergy. Eliminate them during this testing phase.

God in His wisdom has given many useful herbs to aid in healing and nutrition. *"He causeth the grass to grow for the cattle, and herb for the service of man." Psalm 104:14.* In *Revelation 22:2* we read: *"The leaves of the tree were for the healing of the nations."* For this reason herbs may be found to be useful in cleansing and rebuilding the body. Ensure that your source of herbs is of a good quality, free of pesticides and irradiation.

There are many useful herbs for allergies. **Alfalfa**, astragalus, barberry bark, cayenne pepper (capsicum), dandelion, **feverfew**, golden seal (for no longer than 7 days at time and not to be taken by pregnant women), horehound, montmorillonite (bentonite) **clay**, **mullein**, myrrh, plantain, **red clover**, stinging nettles and wild cherry bark are a few. Eucalyptus and/or tea tree oil may be used as an inhalant.

Alfalfa is rich in chlorophyll, astragalus strengthens the body in general, horehound dilates the respiratory vessels while mullein, myrrh and plantain protect the mucous membranes. **Feverfew** provides quercetin, an important antioxidant, which also inhibits mast cells from releasing histamine. Some opt to take supplemental quercetin, but remember food based nutrients have increased bio-availability. Food sources include onions, grapefruit, broccoli, and summer squash. If a supplemental form is chosen, the absorption will be increased with bromelain, the digestive enzyme that is derived from pineapple. Red clover aids in general blood purification. Wild cherry bark is soothing for irritated mucous membranes and clay **adsorbs** substances. **Adsorption** is a process superior to *absorption* in the case of allergens for *absorption* occurs relatively slowly and would allow an allergic reaction, whereas **adsorption** is almost instantaneous, preventing the allergic reaction. Nettles can be helpful for drying out the sinuses. It is also effective for chronic allergies especially when used in the freeze-dried form. This should be used for three to four days, three times a day, and should not be given to children under four.

A fenugreek and thyme tea may be prepared to act as a mild decongestant and relieve congestion in the nasal and sinus region. This can be taken twice a day. Drinking ½ cup of onion tea every 4 hours has eliminated some cases of hay fever. This is made by placing a slice of onion in a quart of water to steep prior to drinking.

The following guidelines will assist you in making food choices in keeping with **GOD'S PLAN:**

1. Avoid refined foods such as:

    Margarine, shortening, refined oil, sugar, syrup, free starch, white bread or bread with unbleached flour, white rice, degerminated corn meal, and store bought meat substitutes such as gluten or soy vegetarian meat

2. Avoid all animal products:

    Meat, fish, fowl, eggs, egg yolks, milk, and milk products such as cheese, butter, cream, ice cream, etc.

3. Avoid these items:

    • Alcoholic beverages, tea, coffee, cola drinks, and beverages containing caffeine.

    • Vinegar containing products such as ketchup, mustard, mayonnaise, pickles, etc.

    • Sprayed, sulfured, or canned (in metal) fruit

    • Canned or frozen juices

    • Peanuts or peanut butter

    • Sprayed or canned vegetables. Fresh is optimal; when not available, frozen is preferable to canned

    • Iceberg lettuce

    • Foods with preservatives and/or food colorings

    • Chewing gum

4. Avoid all of your known trigger foods.

5. Avoid fried food, junk food, and "fast" foods.

6. Avoid foods that you are sensitive to.

7. Limit concentrated foods such as nuts and breads.

THESE FOODS ARE TO BE ENJOYED:

All fresh fruit. Fruit canned in glass or frozen without sugar is the second choice if fresh fruit is not available. If not sensitive to citrus, include the white portion near the peel which is rich in bioflavonoids. Berries when in season along with non-irradiated pineapples are anti-inflammatory.
All greens, especially cabbage, broccoli, turnips, mustards, kale, collards, etc. These are rich in calcium and magnesium. Parsley has properties, which block histamine productions. The Journal of Allergy and Clinical Immunology reports that parsley blocks the formation of histamines, the chemical that triggers allergic attacks. Therefore parsley may assist those who suffer from hay fever or hives.[69] Vegetables should be prepared in a variety of ways, as different nutrients are available by different cooking methods: steamed, raw, stir-fried, baked, etc. If you do eat three meals a day you may find eating two vegetable-based meals is more advantageous than two fruit based meals. Of course, most will find that two meals a day are sufficient.
Fresh spinach, Swiss chard or beet greens may be eaten, but not as freely, due to their oxalate content.
Colorful vegetables, such as carrots, yellow squash, red peppers, eggplant, tomatoes, etc. would also be included if not sensitive to nightshades.
All mild herbs, garlic and onions: Garlic and onions are rich in selenium and sulfur. In addition, garlic stabilizes the mast cells, which contain histamine. Try **kelp** as a seasoning. If it is too "seafood-ish" for you, mix it half-and-half with sea salt.
All legumes: beans, peas, lentils, garbanzos, etc.
All whole grains: Two whole grains combined with one legume daily provide a healthy balance of amino acids. Brown rice, millet, barley, oats, quinoa, amaranth, and buckwheat are some suggestions.
Nuts in moderation: Non-tropical nuts such as almonds, walnuts and pecans tend to be tolerated better.
Seeds, such as sesame, sunflower and pumpkin. Flax seeds contain omega 3 fats, but always grind them prior to use.
Cold pressed oils, such as extra virgin olive oil, flaxseed, evening primrose oil, etc. and oil rich foods such as avocados and olives in moderation.

NOTE: soaking nuts, seeds, legumes and grains prior to use aids in their digestion. An overnight soak prior to use is usually sufficient.

TIPS FOR HEALTHY EATING:

1. 2 fresh fruits daily.
2. A fresh salad daily but limit the number of items allowed on the salad.
3. A dark green or cruciferous vegetable (broccoli, cauliflower, cabbage, brussel sprouts, etc.) should be eaten daily. This may be basis of
   your salad.
4. 2 grains each day
5. 1 legume
6. Tubers, nuts and seeds may be added as desired.

*"Whether therefore ye eat, or drink, or whatsoever ye do, do all to
the glory of God..."
1 Corinthians 10:31.*

21 DAY NUTRITIONAL PROGRAM

This program is designed to assist you in changing from the S.A.D. to G.L.A.D. diet. It involves a short period of fasting which will provide the body with nutrients which are easily assimilated. Fasting also re-educates the taste buds, fortifies the immune system, cleanses the body of toxins as well as gives you more time to meditate on God's word for needed strength in overcome cravings. If (perhaps for medical reasons) you are unable to fast, during the first three days, use the menu for "Day Four." You will receive the benefits, allbeit more slowly.

Follow this program as described below, then refer to "GOD'S PLAN BASIC MENU" as a follow-up menu planner.

Days 1-3

Drink water, lemon water, vegetable juices and potassium broth. Drink at least enough liquids to meet your minimum daily water requirements. To make lemon water, mix 4 oz. freshly squeezed lemon juice with 36 oz. of distilled water. To make vegetable drinks, run the vegetables through a juicer which separates the juice from the pulp. If the juice is too strong, dilute it with distilled water.

Vegetable Drink #1

8 oz. carrot
6 oz. spinach
2 oz. radish

Vegetable Drink #2

8 oz. carrot
3 oz. beet
3 oz. cucumber
2 oz. radish

Vegetable Drink #3

1 oz. of wheat grass juice twice a day, to be taken 30 minutes prior to a vegetable juice or meal.

Potassium Broth:

Blend 1 cup of raw rolled oats with 3 cups of water. Strain liquid and use as a base in which to cook the following vegetables chopped in large pieces.

1 white potato	2 celery stalks
1/3 onion	3 carrots
one handful of parsley	

Cook vegetables until carrots and potatoes are soft enough to be mashed (it is not necessary to mash the vegetables). Strain the liquid and drink the broth.

Day Four

Breakfast: 3-4 servings of raw fruit

Lunch: 2-3 servings of raw vegetables

Optional supper: 1-2 servings of fruit or potassium broth and zwieback

Zwieback
Bake bread slices in the oven at 150 – 200° until crisp. This process changes the bread to an easily digested form.
    *Soak all nuts, grains, seeds and legumes prior to cooking or eating to improve digestion.

Day Five
Breakfast: 2-3 servings of raw fruit with 1 C of millet
Lunch: 2-3 servings of raw vegetables, 1 C of steamed vegetables, 1C rice
Optional supper: Potassium broth and zwieback

Day Six
Begin maintenance and review "Always Temperate" and "Nutrtion". Follow "GOD'S PLAN BASIC MENU."

AVOID
Pressure cooking • microwave cooking • Aluminum cookware (Stainless Steel, Corning Ware, Pyrex glass, or unchipped enamel are best.)

GOD'S PLAN

From S.A.D.
Standard American Diet

To G.L.A.D.
God's Life Activating Diet

Natural Foods Cookbook

GOD'S PLAN BASIC MENU

I. BREAKFAST:
Fresh Fruits: Select 2-3 kinds

<u>**Cooked Grain:**</u> 1 Cup – Choose one of the following: millet, brown rice, quinoa, or amaranth. If not gluten sensitve, oats, barley, buckwheat, spelt, or kamut.

<u>**Fruit Sauce or Spread:**</u> Mix 2 fruits in a blender (optional).

<u>**Almonds:**</u> 8 – 10 (raw)

<u>**Seeds:**</u> 1 Tablespoon (flax seed, raw sunflower, pumpkin, or sesame seeds). Sprinkle ground seeds on salad or grrains.

<u>**Optional Grain, Nut, or Seed Milk:**</u>

Grains
1 Cup cooked grains (millet, rice)
2 – 3 Cups water (to desired consistency)
(optional) pinch of salt
(optional) sweetener
Blend until smooth.

Nuts or Seeds
1 Cup raw nuts or seeds
3 – 4 Cups water (to desired consistency)
Flavorings as above
Blend in a small amount of water until smooth, then add the rest the of water for desired consistency.

II. LUNCH:

Raw Salad: Leaf lettuce, spinach, cabbage, carrots, celery, radishes, green or red peppers, or sprouts, etc.

Steamed vegetables or cooked peas or beans: 1 Cup

Cooked Grain: Choose grain as listed for breakfast, or corn, potato (including skin) baked or steamed, whole grain pasta, or whole grain bread, but limit pastas and breads though.

Basic Salad Dressing: Mix 3 Tbsp. water, juice of one lemon, ½ tsp. onion powder, ¼ tsp. garlic powder, 1 tsp. dried parsley.

Sunflower Seed Dressing: Blend until creamy: 1 2/3 cup water, 1 tsp. salt (optional) ½ tsp. garlic powder, 1 ts.p onion powder, 1 cup sunflower seeds, 1/3 cup lemon juice.

OPTIONAL SUPPER: Potassium broth and zwieback or whole wheat crackers.

GOD'S PLAN DAILY PROGRAM FOR ARRESTING ALLERGIES

6:00 AM   16 oz. warm Lemon Water, Devotion, Deep Breathing
Herbal teas or capsules, Alternating hot/cold shower

7:00 AM   *Leaves of Life Herbal Cleanser*, during the first 3
day of 21 day Nutritional Program, and for the
remainder of the cleansing week as needed. Mix 1 tsp to 4
oz water. (*Leaves of Life Herbal Cleanser* available thru
M.E.E.T. Ministry).

7:30AM   Breakfast - See basic menu plan included in this booklet (for
days 1-3 follow the 21-day nutritional plan).

8:00AM   Take a leisure walk, followed by steam inhalation and nasal
irrigation as indicated.

9:00 AM   During cleanse Sunlight (15-20 minutes), Deep Breathing, then
REST. For maintenance Deep breathing and Sunlight as
schedule allows.

10:00AM   Herbal tea or capsules from M.E.E.T. Ministry

NOON   *Leaves of Life Herbal Cleanser* mix in 1 tsp to 4 oz
water

1:30PM   LUNCH - See basic menu plan included in this
booklet (whilefasting, drink water, juice, or broth)

2:00PM   Take a leisure walk, followed by steam
inhalation and nasal irrigation as indicated.

3:30PM   Herbal tea or capsules from M.E.E.T.

4:30PM   Sunlight - (15 or 20 minutes)

5:30PM   *Leaves of Life Herbal Cleanser,* mix in 1 tsp. to 4
oz. water

6:00PM   Optional Supper - potassium broth or fruit and
zwieback (while fasting, drink water, juice,or broth)

7:00PM   Walk

7:30PM   Devotion, Deep breathing

8:00PM   Warm soak in the bathtub, or other appropriate hydrotherapy
based on symptoms as discussed in "Water"

9:00PM   Bedtime

Power to Change

We *desire* to do better. We know we **must** do better. We even **try** to do better. But all our efforts are as ropes of sand that break with the slightest resistance. We cannot seem to stop eating that ice cream that contains refined sugar. We cannot seem to resist that sirloin steak high in fats and cholesterol.

Multitudes long for a better life, but they lack courage and resolution to break away from the power of habit. They shrink from the effort, struggle and sacrifice demanded, and their lives are wrecked and ruined. But there is hope.

THERE IS POWER TO CHANGE!!

First we must acknowledge that we cannot do it by ourselves. Despite our repeated failures, this is perhaps the hardest step. We all like to believe we can do it by ourselves, that we don't need any help. But we need a Power above and beyond ourselves in order to change our life-style and live a healthy, happy life. And that power is Christ Jesus.

When we realize we cannot do it ourselves, we can then go to Christ for help. He will supply the power be-  cause He has promised to do so in *Matthew 28:18*, "All power is given unto me in Heaven and in earth." Indeed, your very desire to change is proof that He is ready, willing, wanting and able to provide you with all the power to change, "For it is God which worketh in you both to will and to do of His good pleasure." (Philippians 2:13).

Next, we must trust God that He will do what He says. This is faith, and "without faith it is impossible to please Him: for He that cometh to God must believe that He is, and that He is a rewarder of them that diligently seek Him." (Hebrews 11:6).

As we trust Him, as we put our faith in Him and not in ourselves, we must then step out in faith and not violate His laws of health. Jesus gives us strength to do this only one day at a time: "...as thy days, so shall thy strength be." (Deuteronomy 33:25).

Although all the power is His, the decision to avail ourselves of His power always remains with us. As the children of Israel before they entered the earthly Canaan, you must "Choose you this day whom ye will serve; whether the gods which your fathers served that were on the other side of the flood, or the gods of the Amorites, in whose land ye dwell [which included the "gods" of feasting, intemperance, and appetite]: but as for me and my house, we will serve the Lord" (Joshua 24:15). We must choose to serve the Lord if we are to enter the Heavenly Canaan.

A lesson from nature illustrates the power of our Creator God to affect change.

The caterpillar is probably not one of the world's most beautiful creatures, yet the caterpillar has the potential to be transformed into an exquisite butterfly. The actual term for the transformation of a caterpillar to a butterfly is the Greek word *metamorphosis*. Paul used this same Greek word which we translate as transformed in *Romans 12:2*: "...be transformed by the renewing of your mind, that you may prove what is that good and acceptable and perfect will of God."

This transformation starts with an action of the mind, a conscious decision. Everything depends on Godly thoughts and thinking patterns because they have the ability to transform our habits and actions according to God's Plan "for as he thinketh in his heart, so is he." (Proverbs 23:7).

We must make a searching and fearless inventory of our habits and life-style, admitting to God and ourselves the exact nature of our wrongs, humbly asking God to remove our shortcomings, being entirely ready for Him to work in us and for us.

Let's look at another important picture from nature that mirrors what happens when we work together with God in following His plan for our health and happiness. This picture is of something that happens in every cell in our body.

Imagine a typical cell in our body by thinking of a circle. Attached to the outside of this circle are a number of receptor points.

Floating around near the cell are hormones and enzymes that have indentations that exactly fit the shape of the receptor points. When a hormone or enzyme grasps hold of a receptor point, it has a special ability to stimulate a cell's activity. This stimulation is called "positive cooperativety".

When we cooperate with God by receiving His power, our bodies and minds are stimulated to activity in following His health laws. When the temptation comes to eat or do anything that will violate the laws of God, we must pray and ask God for the power to resist. And then, knowing that He has heard and answered our petitions, we **must** walk away. We **must** push away that plate of dainties. We **must** honor God by removing ourselves from the temptation as far and as often as possible. Once we do this, it becomes easier for us to repeat this action.

Through prayer and meditation on God's Word, we improve our conscious contact with Him. Thus we are better able to understand His will for us and can avail ourselves of the power which He so freely offers us.

In all this, and through this, we will learn to love the Lord and love Him more. God has promised, "Whereby are given unto us exceeding great and precious promises: that **by these ye might be partakers of the divine nature**, having escaped the corruption that is in the world through lust (2 Peter 1:4, emphasis added)." And what is the divine nature but a nature of divine love, for "God is love" (see 1 John 4:18, 19).

Loving obedience to God's laws of health results in the restoration of a measure of health for a better life here and a preparation for eternal life with Him forever. Although all the power is God's, the decision to use it lies with us. The miracle is that GOD'S PLAN for our lives works. It may not be fully explained, but it can be fully experienced.

God has pledged Himself to keep this human machinery in healthful action if the human agent will obey His laws and cooperate with God.

As you cooperate with God, you will be convinced that: G.O.D.S. P.L.A.N. can ARREST your ALLERGIES !!!!!!!!!!

COME ASIDE AND REST AWHILE

M.E.E.T. Ministry has developed a home-like health center in the peaceful countryside of West Tennessee. We call the center *Our Home* Health Center. It provides an 18-day program designed specifically to meet the physical and spiritual needs of each guest. These needs may include systemic illnesses such as cancer, diabetes, hypertension, arthritis, obesity and lupus. Our experienced staff also counsels in the areas of stress management, depression, substance abuse, as well as overcoming smoking.

Each day our guests are educated through instructional classes. They learn how to prepare nutritious and appetizing vegetarian meals. We instruct them in the concept of GOD'S PLAN, what it is and how to apply it to their everyday lives. Juice therapy, herbal therapy, hydrotherapy, massage, along with outdoor exercise in the garden are incorporated into each session.

Upon completion of the 18-day program, each guest not only begins to learn how to cooperate with God for physical restoration, but they also have found new family members whom they cherish.

If you or someone you know would like to come aside and rest awhile and take advantage of what we offer at *Our Home*, please contact us at least three weeks in advance of the starting date.

M.E.E.T. Ministry, 480 Neely Lane, Huntingdon, TN 38344
(731) 986-3518, FAX (731) 986-0582
E-mail: godsplan@meetministry.org
Web Site: www.meetministry.org

Would You Like to M.E.E.T.?

WHAT IS M.E.E.T. MINISTRY?
MISSIONARY EDUCATION AND EVANGELISTIC TRAINING

M.E.E.T. Ministry is a Christian health ministry. We believe from inspiration and research that most of our sickness is the result of our departure from G.O.D.'S. P.L.A.N. and that only in obedience to the laws of God, both natural and spiritual, can true health be restored or preserved. Our ministry conducts health seminars of varying duration, along with cooking schools and training workshops. Our focus is "training," and with God's help, we seek to prepare others to be health missionaries. Our training culminates with a four month training school held once a year on our country property in Tennessee. M.E.E.T. is a self-supporting ministry. Although we do accept donations, we seek to sustain our ministry with industries which provide income and bless the community as well.

We would love to MEET you! If you would like to schedule a seminar for your church, social group, etc., we would love to come and share how GOD'S PLAN affects, obesity, arthritis, drug addictions of all kinds, and every other ailment which is bringing suffering and death to millions everyday. So how do we MEET? Just contact our office for details. It's that simple!

M.E.E.T. Ministry, 480 Neely Lane, Huntingdon, TN 38344
(731) 986-3518, FAX (731) 986-0582
E-mail: godsplan@meetministry.org
Web Site: www.meetministry.org

Bibliography

Aihara, Herman, *Acid and Alkaline,* George Ohsawa Macrobiotic
    Foundation, Oroville, CA 1986.
Austin, Phyllis, and Agatha and Calvin Thrash, M.D., *Food Allergies
    Made Simple,* Family Health Publications, Sunfield, MI 1985.
————, *Natural Healthcare for Your Child,* Family Health
    Publications, Sunfield, MI, 1990.
Balch, James F., M.D. and Phyllis A. Balch, *Prescription for
    Nutritional Healing,* Avery Publishing Group, Garden City Park,
    NY 1997.
Barney, Paul, M.D., *Doctor's Guide to Natural Medicine,* Woodland
    Publishing, Pleasant Grove, UT, 1998.
Bateson-Koch, Carolee, D.C., N.D., *Allergies: Disease in Disguise,*
    Alive Books, Burnaby, BC, Canada, 1994.
Bragg, Paul C., N.D. Ph.D and Patricia Bragg N.D. Ph.D., *Bragg
    Healthy Lifestyle,* Health Science, Santa Barbara, CA 1999.
Broadhurst, C. Leigh., Ph.D., *Natural Relief from Asthma,* Alive Books,
    Vancouver, Canada, 2000.
Brown, H. Morrow, M.D., *All About Asthma and Allergy,* The Crowood
    Press, Wiltshire,1990.
Carlisle, Norman and Madelyn, *Where to Life For Your Health,*
    Harcourt Brace Jovanovich, New York, NY 1980.
Cooper, Kenneth, *Advanced Nutritional Therapies,* Thomas Nelson
    Inc., Nashville, TN 1996.
Crook, William G., M.D., *The Yeast Connection Handbook,*
Professional   Books, Jackson, TN 1997.
Dail, Clarence W., M.D. and Charles S. Thomas, M.D., *Simple
    Remedies for the Home,* MMI Press, Harrisville, NH 1985.
Ferrell, Vance, *The Natural Remedies Encyclopedia,* Harvestime
    Books Altamont, TN, 1998.
Foster, Vernon W., M.D., *New Start,* Woodbridge Press, Santa Barbara,
    CA, 1989.
Ganong, W.F., M.D., *Medical Physiology,* Lange Medical Publishing,
    Los Altos, CA, 1985.
Glassburn, Vicky, *Who Killed Candida,* Teach Services, Brushton, NY
    1991.
Hart, Archibald D., M.D., *The Hidden Link Between Adrenaline and
    Stress,* Word Publishing, Dallas, TX 1995.

Human Anatomy and Physiology, 2nd Edition, Wm. C Brown Company Publishers, Dubuque, IA 1981.

Kail, Konrad, N.D. and Bobbi Lawrence with Bruce Goldberg, *Allergy Free,* AlternativeMedicine.com, Inc., Tiburon, CA 2000.

Kaufmann, Doug A. *The Fungus Link*, Media Trition, Rockwall, TX, 2000.

Kime, Zane, M.D. M.S. *Sunlight Could Save your Life,* World Health Publications, Penryn, CA 1980.

Jack, Alex, *Let Food be thy Medicine,* One Peaceful World, Becket, MA 1994.

Huggins, Hal, M.D., *It's all in your Head,* Avery Publishing, Garden City Park, NY 1993.

Ivker, Robert S., *Sinus Survival,* Penguin Putnam Inc., New York, NY 2000.

Ludington, Aileen, M.D. and Hans Diehl, M.D., *Health Power,* Review and Herald Publishing, Hagerstown, MD 2000.

Murray, Michael N.D. and Joseph Pizzorno N.D., *Encyclopedia of Natural Medicine,* Prima Publishing, Rocklin, CA 1991.

Paulien, Gunther B., Ph.d., *The Divinie Philosophy and Science of Health and Healing,* Teach Services, Brushton, NY 1995.

Page, Linda Rector., N.D., PhD., *Healthy Healing,* Publications, www.healthyhealing.com, 1997.

Pedersen, Mark, *Nutritional Herbology,* Wendell Whitman Co., Warsaw, IN, 1994.

Taber's Cyclopedic Medical Dictionary, 15th Edition, FA Davis Company, Philadelphia, PA 1985.

Thrash, Agatha and Calvin M.D.'s, *Home Remedies,* Yuchi Pines Institute, Seale, AL, 1981.

Trivier, Larry Jr., and John W. Anderson, Eds., *Alternative Medicine, The Definitive Guide,* Celestial Arts, Berkeley, CA 2002.

Werbach, Melvyn R. M.D., *Nutritional Influences on Illness,* Kits Publishing, Inc., New Canaan, CT, 1988.

Walker, N.W., *Fresh Vegetable and Fruit Juices,* Norwalk Press, Prescott, AZ, 1976.

(Footnotes)

1   http://www.niaid.nih.gov/factsheets/allergystat.htm.
2   http://hlm.nih/govmedlineplus/ency/article/00813.htm.
3   http://www.niaid.nih.gov/factsheets/allergystat.htm.
4   http://mywebmd.com/content/article/11680.5011.
5   Kail, Konrad, *Allergy Free,* p 14.
6   Austin, Phyllis, *Food Allergies Made Simple* p 53
7   http://www.niaid.nih.gov/factsheets/allergystat.htm.
8   http://www.energy medic.co.uk/allergy_stats.htm.
9   http://www.energy medic.co.uk/allergy_stats.htm.
10 Murray, Michael N.D., *Encyclopedia of Natural Medicine* p. 305.
11 Time *"A Kiss Before Sneezing"* 6/17/02 or www.time.com/archive/preview/
     0,10987,1002680,00.html.
12 Bragg, Paul C., N.D. Ph.D., *Bragg Healthy Lifestyle,* p 2.
13 http://mywebmd.com/content/asset/adam_disease_allergies.
14 http//mywebmd.com/content/pages/10/1625_50536?z.
15 Bateson-Koch, Carolee, D.C., N.D., *Allergies: Disease in Disguise,* p 15-19.
16 *Taber's Cyclopedic Medical Dictionary,* 15th Edition, p 60
17 *Human Anatomy and Physiology,* 2nd Edition, p 101, 637,638
18 Bateson-Koch p 27.
19 Page, Linda Rector., N.D., Ph.D., *Healthy Healing,* p 230.
20 Murray, p 330.
21 Austin, *Food Allergies,* p 49, 50.
22 Austin, Phyllis, *Natural Healthcare for Your Child* p 105.
23 Jack, Alex, *Let Food be thy Medicine,* p 78.
24 Austin, *Food Allergies,* p 47.
25 Kail, p 14.
26 Bateson-Koch p 9.
27 Austin, *Food Allergies* p 7,8.
28 Ibid., p 7, 8.
29 Kaufmann, Doug A. *The Fungus Link*, p 58.
30 ww.bt.cdc.gov/agent/agentistchem.asp.
31 http://my.webmd.com/content/article/60/66968.htm..
32 http://my.webmd.com/content/article/35/1625_52222.htm.
33 Page, p 230, 85, 194.
34 Wilson, James L., N.D., D.C., Ph.D., *Adrenal Fatigue,* p 249.
35 Werbach, Melvyn R. M.D., *Nutritional Influences on Illness,* p 27.
36 Bateson-Koch p 60.
37 Kaufmann, p 83.
38 Broadhurst, C. Leigh., Ph.D., *Natural Relief from Asthma,* p 31.
39 Bateson-Koch p 45, 46.
40 Austin, *Food Allergies* p 8.
41 Bateson-Koch p 42.

42 Ibid. p 92.
43 Ibid. p 98.
44 Austin, Food Allergies, p 9, 10.
45 Journal of Health & Healing v 20, #3 p 15.
46 Austin, *Food Allergies* p 35.
47 Austin, *Food Allergies,* p 17.
48 Bateson-Koch p 145.
49 Cooper, Kenneth, M.D., *Advanced Nutritional Therapy,* p 85, 86.
50 Murray, p 368.
51 Bateson-Koch p 157
52 Clinical News 10/2001 p 18.
53 Braggs, p 5.
54 Kail, p 359.
55 Kail, p 351, 352.
56 Aihara, Herman, *Acid and Alkaline,* p 96.
57 Carlisle, Norman and Madelyn, *Where to Life for Your Health,* p 71, 72.
58 htpp://www.surroundair.com/ion-ozone.htm
59 Carlisle, p 71, 72.
60 Paulien, Gunther B., Ph.D., *The Divine Philosophy and Science of Health and Healing,* p 91.
61 Ivker, Robert S., *Sinus Survival,* p 105 and Kail, p 260.
62 Ibid. p 114.
63 Ibid. p 113.
64 Foster, Vernon W., M.D., *New Start,* p 44.
65 Kime, Zane, M.D. M.S. *Sunlight Could Save your Life,* p 243, 234.
66 Kail, p 40.
67 Balch, James F., M.D., *Prescription for Nutritional Healing,* p 112, 298.
68 Kail, p 83.
69 Ward, Bernard, *Healing Foods from the Bible,* p 53.

Notes

Made in the USA
Columbia, SC
20 September 2023

23105375R00043